# WHAT GOD HAS JOINED TOGETHER!

BONITA L. REYNOLDS

# What God has Joined Together

BoNita L. Reynolds



Scripture quotations, unless otherwise noted, are taken from  THE HOLY BIBLE, King James Version (KJV). Cambridge Edition 1769. Used by permission. All rights reserved worldwide. Or are taken from the Holy Bible, New International Version®, NIV®. Copyright © 1973, 1978, 1984, 2011 by Biblica, Inc.TM Used by permission of Zondervan. All rights reserved worldwide. www.zondervan.com. The "NIV" and "New International Version" are trademarks registered in the United States Patent and Trademark Office by Biblica, Inc.TM

This is an autobiographical work, and stories, observations, anecdotes, and memories are to the best of the author's recollection or as shared with her.

Published by Pecan Tree Publishing
Hollywood, FL 33020
www.pecantreebooks.com
info@pecantreebooks.com

ISBN: 979-8-9938089-0-1  Paperback
ISBN: 979-8-9938089-1-8 Ebook

Library of Congress Control Number: On file

Edited by: E. Claudette Freeman
Interior and Cover Design by: Charlyne Strachan
Author Photo by: JC Penney

# DEDICATION

I dedicate this book to my husband, Darnell.

I would not have been able to complete the book without your love and support.

Thank You, Babe.

# CONTENTS

# ACKNOWLEDGEMENTS

Thank you, Kim Waddy, for encouraging me to write this book.

Special thanks to Regina Hodges, who helped with the book and encouraged me as well.

Thanks to Phyllis Chestnut, Minnie Coleman, Michelle Conerly, and Arlece Welton for your support, love, and guidance in telling me what was right and wrong.

Thank you, and I love you all.

# INTRODUCTION

# Before We Get Into Marriage

I WAS BORN IN 1956 AT Holy Family Hospital, which was built in 1943 by the Catholic religion as part of the Black Hospital Movement during segregation.

I grew up in Homewood, which is a suburb of Birmingham, Alabama, in Jefferson County. We lived in a small beige duplex down the street from the ball diamond or baseball field. My Dad had a Little League baseball team, and one of his players later became an Original Commodore (the R&B group). His name is William King, but back in the day, they called him Butch.

Family surrounded me on both my father's and my mother's sides. We would meet at my grandparents' house on my mom's side on Friday night and stay until Sunday after dinner. The adults would be outside selling barbecue dinners, and the kids would be playing inside. My Uncle Lawrence (we all called him Big Lawrence) would buy a big box of corn flakes, pork and beans, and wieners, which was what we kids would eat. We could not wait for Friday night to come!

We also spent a lot of time with my grandmother. Some of the games we would play were Mother May I, Red Light, Green Light, Paddle Ball, Jacks, Jump Rope, Hopscotch, Four Square, and Marbles. We would have a "Tom Thumb Wedding" at the church my dad attended, "Union Baptist Church," which was right across the street from my grandparents' home. My mom's side of the family attended Homewood Church of God, which was about a 15-minute walk away.

At the age of three, almost four, I sang my first solo, "I Come To The Garden Alone," at my dad's church. My grandmother helped me learn the whole song within a week. When the next Sunday came, they called my name, and I went up to the mic and began to sing. The musician was a young man named Alphonso. He was on the organ. I asked him to stop the music and follow me. I received a standing ovation. That was the start of my singing in church.

From my grandmother's back door, you could see the statue, Vulcan. It is made of cast iron and is the symbol of Birmingham, which was known for its iron and steel industry back in the day. It is the world's largest statue and the tallest in the nation. Vulcan is on top of Red Mountain Park in Alabama, now called Vulcan Park and Museum. In May of 2007, Vulcan Park and Museum became the official information center for the city of Birmingham. My great-granddad and our family are mentioned in the museum.

I was five years old when my family moved to California. My dad, uncle, and two of their friends drove out to California about two months before we did. My parents wanted to provide a better life for my siblings and me. My mom, my siblings, and I came out to California on the Southern Pacific train. We were so excited to see my dad as soon as we stepped off the train, and he gave us all big hugs!

I had an awesome childhood that most children often dream about. We lived with my dad's sister, Aunt Mary, her husband,

Uncle Allen, and their granddaughter, Mal, in San Gabriel. My sister Nita and I attended school in San Gabriel before moving to Los Angeles, off First Street. We then attended Utah Street School. My teacher, Ms. Bumstead, was awesome! We would have spelling and math tests, and whoever had 100 on both tests was invited to spend the weekend with her. There were only four of us: three girls and one boy. She took us to Chinatown, and we played spelling and math games. She even let us do her hair! I had the time of my life.

While living in Los Angeles, we attended Wadsworth Church of God. After moving to Compton, I attended Victory Park Elementary and attended Compton First Church of God. After living on Palm Street for two years, we moved to South Clymar Ave. I would then attend Charles W. Burch Elementary, Enterprise Junior High School, and Compton Senior High School.

While in the 11th and 12th grades, I attended Los Angeles Trade Technical on Saturday for Fashion Design and Typing. On Wednesday nights, I went to McDonnell Douglas Aircraft for Computer Programming, which was my way of getting out of church!

The pastor of our church was Clovis Wellington. I remember my dad asking him to show him in the bible and explain to him why he should not smoke or drink. Dad said he was the first pastor to ever explain it to him. My Dad put his cigarettes down and never smoked again in his life. I don't remember my dad drinking, but he said he did. My dad became a member of Compton First Church of God, and he and my mother were ordained as deacons.

We were attending Compton First Church of God. It seemed like we were in church every time the doors opened! Daddy was the Sunday school superintendent, and to get out of going to Sunday school, I would help him. My parents both sang in the choir, and we were also church janitors. Each family took turns cleaning the church each weekend, and even when they were unable to, my father volunteered to make sure it was done for our family.

I started working at 12, as a bottle capper at Max Factor in Gardena, CA, during the summer. I wasn't very tall, so I had to stand on a milk crate! I started working so I could buy the things I wanted without having to ask my parents for anything. The following summer, my friend Michelle worked there with me.

I graduated from high school in 1974. The graduation ceremony was held on a Thursday night, and the following Monday, I started at Bryman School of Nursing, where I finished in October. It was hard, however, to find work in the nursing field, as I was either too short or too Black. WOW!

I took a job at J. C. Penney's in the toy department. In December 1974, the Family Health Program called me for an interview. I was hired on the spot. I started at the appointment center, then moved to the back office. After bruising an elderly lady's arm, I realized I had been heavy-handed and asked to be transferred to the front desk, where I worked as a receptionist. I enjoyed being a receptionist. I loved the paperwork and the rush of completing my work on time. I would finish my paperwork and help others.

My boss at that time was Barbara Fish. She asked me if I wanted to work as a floater. I took her up on the offer, and whenever someone was absent, I would fill in and travel to other locations. My home base was in Long Beach.

Having a great job, I was able to purchase my first car all by myself from the Toyota dealership in Long Beach. I traded in my gold Toyota Corolla, which was bought for my older sister Anita when she married Ed Carey in 1972, and it was passed down to me. I purchased a brown 1974 Toyota Corolla. It had gold stripes, and I named her Brown Sugar!

That is the story of my beginning. But that's not what we will talk about in this book. We will talk about my experience with relationships and marriage. I am going to talk about some things that I hope will help you. I will share my story, my faith, my hurt, my lessons, and the scripture that helped me, and I know will help you.

# CHAPTER 1

# *What God Says About Marriage*

I WAS DISCUSSING WITH SOMEONE WHAT my earliest understanding of marriage was, whether it came from the church or my family. I was about 10 years of age when I heard our pastor preach on marriage and divorce. When I got home, I questioned my parents about it. My dad explained that God wanted a man to marry a woman, not to live together, because living together is a sin. "He who finds a wife finds a good thing" (Proverbs 18:22).

I asked the question, "How will he know a good thing from a bad thing?"

My mom said we would talk about it more when I was old enough to understand.

My first views on marriage, though I don't remember developing until I was about 17. God views marriage as a sacred covenant between a man and a woman; He ordained it to be a lifelong, exclusive union. Ephesians 5:25 states that "Husbands should love their wives, just as Christ loved the church and gave himself up for her." In 1 Corinthians 13:4-8, "Love is patient and kind; love does not envy or boast; it is not arrogant or rude." Mark 10:9 states,

1

"Therefore what God has joined together, let no man separate," just to name a few verses.

I was 17, and we were at my aunt's church in Pomona, California, when the pastor was teaching about marriage and divorce. This was on a Wednesday night. He asked if there were any questions.

I told him I would like to elaborate on what he said, based on what I'd been taught, and gave him scriptures to back up what I was saying. What I shared was that you can't simply say you no longer love your spouse or that you're divorcing them. I said the Bible states, "What God has joined together, let no man put asunder." I said that just because you do not love your spouse, it doesn't mean you should try to rekindle your relationship. It should be "graveyard dead," not "love dead," as my mom would say.

I gave him the following scriptures, and different members of my aunt's church were reading them and going along with what the Bible said.

Corinthians 7:1-40, 1 Peter 3:1-5

Corinthians 6:14, 1 Corinthians 7:39

Ephesians 5:22-33, 1 Peter 3:7

1 Peter 4:8, Proverbs 19:14

Proverbs 21:9, Ephesians 5:25

Genesis 2:18, Malachi 2:13-16

Matthew 19:2-12, Colossians 3:18-19

My aunt said, "You really know what you're talking about."

I said, "I should. Pastor Wellington preached on this subject for as long as I can remember."

My aunt said we may not be able to come back to this church. My aunt's pastor asked me if I was in the ministry. I said no, our pastor just preached on this subject a lot. We later found out that the pastor in Pomona and his wife had gotten divorced.

My parents were a great example of a beautiful marriage. I'm sure that they didn't agree on everything. We could tell if my mom was upset; she would be in the kitchen humming. They never discussed anything in front of us girls. They would always talk in their bedroom.

In my opinion, "one flesh" means that the unity of one flesh in marriage reflects the relationship between Christ and the church. It is the unity and intimacy of marriage; you become one. We may not agree on everything, but we can come to an understanding and not let the sun go down on your wrath (Ephesians 4:26), which means do not go to bed angry. Get the situation under control before you go to sleep. Tomorrow is not promised.

Faith provides the foundation for submission, and it helps your spouse to trust in God's plan for your marriage. "Faith is the substance of things hoped for, the evidence of things not seen" (Hebrews 11:1). Submission is respect and honor for God's plan in your marriage. It's providing a framework for mutual respect, love, and support, grounded in a belief in God's design for marriage. Submission, in this context, isn't about one spouse being dominated but about both spouses choosing to prioritize their relationship with God and each other, having the same relationship as between Christ and the church. This will help you navigate challenges and make wise decisions together. Faith is a foundation in marriage that helps you with major decisions, difficult times, and disagreements, and helps you stay at peace with each other.

The Bible states that the wife should submit to her husband, but it also emphasizes that both spouses should submit to one another. This is honoring and respecting each other's roles and contributions to marriage. You should never use submission against each other.

As we continue to talk about how our church taught or modeled marital roles, our pastor preached on marriage and divorce. He stated that you should not get a divorce, for it is against God's will. Again, my role models were my parents. Many churches teach that the husband is the head of the family, as Christ is the head of the church. The 5th chapter of Ephesians and the 11th chapter of 1 Corinthians outline the roles of the husband and the wife.

Our pastor preached on divorce for as long as I can remember. Each married couple that attended our church was together until death did them part. It's ironic now that I think about it. Both of our pastor's daughters divorced their husbands.

The very first time I heard the term "'til death do us part" was when my mom said it to someone on the phone. We were not allowed to get into grown-ups' conversations, so I never asked her what that meant. Then I started to hear it at weddings. I'm not sure if my mom said it first or if I heard it at a wedding first.

God's covenant involves unconditional love and grace, whereas legal contracts focus on obligations and reciprocal exchanges. A contract focuses on benefit and obligation. In marriage, there is no contract. A covenant, yes, because it is forever, whereas a contract is for a limited time only. Marriage is viewed as a sacred covenant between a man and a woman, ordained by God to be a lifelong, exclusive union. Scriptures emphasize love, respect, and submission within marriage. I have listed just a few below; please read them.

Not only did I read scriptures, but I also listened to songs. The scriptures that guided me are:

Ephesians 5:25: "Husbands, love your wives, just as Christ loved the church and gave himself up for her."

Psalms 121:1-2: "I will lift my eyes unto the hills, from whence cometh my help. My help cometh from the Lord, which made heaven and earth."

1 Corinthians 13:4-7: "Charity suffereth long, and is kind; charity envieth not; charity vaunteth not itself, is not puffed up. Doth not behave itself unseemly, seeketh not her own, is not easily provoked, thinketh no evil; Rejoiceth not in iniquity, but rejoiceth in the truth; Beareth all things, believeth all things, hopeth all things, endureth all things."

1 Peter 4:8: "Above all, love each other deeply, because love covers over a multitude of sins."

Mark 10:9: "What God has joined together, let no man separate."

Some of the music that soothed me and provided wisdom were:

"'Tis So Sweet to Trust in Jesus"

"God's Woman"

"Keep Praying, Toiling on"

"My Faith Looks Up to Thee"

"Where Is Your Faith in God"

"God Will Take Care of You"

"Lord, Help Me to Hold Out"

"Alabaster Box"

Grace plays a fundamental role in marriage. With grace, you can build a strong and healthy relationship with your spouse. Grace will give you undeserved favor, love, and forgiveness; you are looking beyond their flaws and remembering why you love them.

My grandmother would always say, "Baby, he was not brought up in this household. Not everyone was brought up like you. Baby, he's doing the best that he can. Please keep him in your prayers and in your heart. You keep living your life in front of him, and a change will come. He has good potential. God is working on him; let God do his thing."

Some believe that marriage is outdated, and that a marriage that forgives faults is outdated. Although those ideas are popular these days, for me, it is not a matter of debate. As a Christian, if you really believe in the Word, living together is against God's will. Some people say they would not get married because it did not work for their parents and grandparents. They say marriage is too much trouble and a pain, and that living together is more practical. Marriage is viewed as a sacred covenant between a man and a woman, clearly ordained by God to be a lifelong and exclusive love. Scripture emphasizes love, respect, and submission within marriage, reflecting the unity between Christ and the church.

The practicality of living together before marriage varies widely depending on individual beliefs, cultural norms, and personal circumstances. Some people find it more practical because it allows them to understand their partner's habits, compatibility, and lifestyle before making a lifelong commitment. This can help in making a more informed decision about marriage. When living together before marriage, you have less commitment and responsibility, and it harms your morals, such as with premarital sex and your commitment to each other. This is just my opinion.

Ultimately, the key is to find what works best for you and your partner and to respect each other's beliefs and values. Open communication and mutual understanding are essential in any relationship.

God has given us three purposes for marriage:

**Companionship:** In Genesis 2:18, the Lord said it was not good for man to be alone. God designed marriage so that man and woman could have a close relationship. As I have stated, the relationship should be based on love, trust, and communication. Love, far too often, leaves marriage, as does trust; we cannot trust our partners. We go through their phone, listen to their messages and conversations, check out their social media pages and pictures, go into their drawers, and go through their car. Oh my God, that is just too much work to do, and please don't come home late. There will be 50 million questions.

**Procreation:** God designed marriage so couples could have children and raise them in loving homes. Children are a blessing from God. Parents, please raise your children in a loving, caring, guiding, and nurturing home. Tell them about the love of God. If you seek God first, then family, you will succeed in raising your family in a God-based home. God first, then family; the husband is the head of the house. If your husband is not fulfilling his duties or responsibilities, the wife will take them on.

**Redemption:** God designed marriage so that man and woman could come together and be saved from their sins. When you say, "I do," you not only make a commitment to each other, but you also make one to God.

The three purposes for marriage are still relevant in today's world.

# CHAPTER 2

## *The Marriage Vows Still Matter*

WEDDING VOWS, TO ME, ARE sacred promises that bind two souls together in an unbreakable union. The words spoken during the ceremony form the foundation of a lifelong commitment. When I said my vows, I did so with utmost seriousness and dedication: a lifelong commitment between two people, expressing love, loyalty, faithfulness, trust, honesty, and a shared vision between a husband and his wife.

My vows were really tested when I was faced with a challenging situation involving infidelity and an unexpected pregnancy. It was not the vows that were being tested, but the commitment they represent, which is often tested by various life challenges. Your vows can be tested in a relational sense as follows:

- Life's Challenges
- Commitment and Growth
- Communication and Trust
- Personal and Social Expectations

Wedding vows are not simply words spoken on a day-to-day basis, but a strong foundation upon which a husband and wife build their relationship. All right, tell me what husband and wife you know could do the things that they promise to do at their wedding ceremony. Never hold your spouse's weaknesses against them, such as their inability to make more money.

My most challenging part of the vows to live out was "to love and to cherish." If you love and cherish, it signifies that you will hold fast to the commitment to deeply care for and value your relationship. It was difficult to maintain love, trust, and submission, and keep a straight face amidst my hurt and pain. To me, he did not take our vows as seriously as I did. It was hard for me to be kind, pleasant, and loving when you betrayed me by having an affair while we were married. I felt as if our marriage was a joke to him, if you have to go out and have an affair with who knows how many women. You could have just told me, and I would have let you go.

I had so many women calling me about affairs with my husband over the years. So would brag about how good he was in the bedroom. Some would tell me they were pregnant with his child. I just ignored those calls.

Honestly, at one point, I really wanted to take my vows back, especially when it came to his infidelity. Marriage really isn't about making the vows; the problem is keeping the vows that you said before God and man. The infidelity took me over the top. I told my pastor I wanted a divorce. My husband was married to the streets. He told me he loved me; he did not know how to show it. That was not helping me at all.

Yes, people go back on their words and break their promises. The thing is, he should have just called it off if he wasn't ready to take the leap. He asked me to marry him three times; I did not ask him to marry me. I went into our marriage with the intention of it lasting forever. He showed all the signs of being a happy and loving person before we got married. He took care of me; whatever he thought I wanted, he got it for me.

I really did not want people to mock or question my commitment, because I did not want them to know how stupid I was for putting up with him. Only one who knew was my mom, and I'm sure my grandmother knew something was going on; she was waiting for me to tell her. Before I got married, some friends said they didn't think it would last.

I questioned my commitment myself. He betrayed our commitment when he was not honest about what he most likely cared about; as you are reading, it was not me. My starting place was often question-asking, problem-posting, and inner-seeking. I notice if any of these resonate with me, I have a place to reflect on and pray about my situation.

It was hard for me to recommit after being betrayed. It took a lot of prayers for me to recommit myself to him. I wanted him dead and her as well. I had to start processing my emotions and rebuilding trust in myself before I could trust someone else. I acknowledged and validated my feelings of hurt, anger, sadness, and confusion, as well as other emotions. I even began to blame myself for his infidelity.

We sought counseling to rekindle our relationship by revisiting activities we enjoyed together early on. We began taking walks, going out to dinner, and just spending time together.

I'm not sure that my husband understood or valued the vows the way I did. He stated he understood and valued the vows, but his actions spoke louder than his words. His not understanding it potentially led to misunderstandings and disappointment later on in our marriage. In my opinion, I really don't think he was truly committed to the vows as much as I was. I do not believe he was in his right state of mind. I emphasized love and honor, while my husband was emphasizing something altogether different.

I really do not think that if we had written our own vows, it would have mattered. God has held me accountable for our vows. Failing to fulfill our vows is considered a sin, and the consequences can range from repercussions to real-world consequences. Our vows are a solemn promise made to God and breaking them is considered a form of sin in God's eyes. The vows are a covenant between God and me, and breaking our vows is a breach of trust with God. Making a vow to God is viewed as a sacred act, a solemn commitment to fulfill a specific action. While breaking a vow has consequences, the Bible also offers avenues for repentance, forgiveness, and restoration. God's accountability regarding vows is a core concept in many religious traditions, emphasizing the seriousness and binding nature of promises made to Him.

In other words, our religious fervor, and the grace we receive from God in prayer may move us to make a vow to God. Vows are serious, solemn commitments, and we do not want to make a vow that we may end up breaking. We stood before men and God to say our vows, and then we broke them.

Spiritual counseling impacts your perspective. Spiritual counseling gets deeply into your emotional pain through kindness and compassion. It also helped us to remember to forgive. Spiritual counseling, particularly faith-based counseling, can significantly impact a person's perspective by providing moral and ethical guidance, fostering spiritual growth, and promoting overall well-being. It helps individuals connect with their faith, find meaning in life, and helps us cope with life's challenges through a holistic approach that combines mental health support with spiritual practices. Counseling can help deepen your relationship with God through prayer and praying together. As we began counseling, I understood my emotional pain through the eyes of kindness and compassion.

Many counseling professionals believe that spiritual beliefs and practices can significantly impact our overall well-being. Our counselor was related to me and was a Christian, so you know she had us doing things by the Bible. I figured that since she was my cousin, she would be on my side. Not a chance. She had us pray before and after each session. The benefits of a Christian counselor were very helpful to us. She would have us write down what we loved about each other, then write down the things we didn't like about each other. We could not use profanity while in her presence, which was a good thing. I do not use profanity at all.

If we have faith at the heart of our healing journey, we will find greater resilience and a stronger sense of self. She was able to bring out a lot that my husband had never told me about his life. It gave me a clearer understanding of him and what he was going through.

Keeping our vows is a reward in itself. You start with a closer relationship with God and your spouse. Keeping your vows in marriage strengthens your relationship and integrity and has a positive impact on your own life. Faithfulness in fulfilling promises can lead to deeper trust, enhanced self-respect, and a sense of peace knowing you have honored your commitment to each other and God. Keeping your vows helps you build trust with your spouse and build a strong, lasting relationship. Your commitment to keeping your vows can inspire others to do the same and contribute to a more trustworthy, stable society.

Keeping your vows aligns with societal expectations and norms, contributing to social cohesion. Honoring your commitments can lead to a sense of fulfillment and emotional stability. Also, breaking your vows can result in guilt, regret, and anxiety, while keeping them can enhance your overall well-being.

"When you make a vow to God, do not delay fulfilling it. He has no pleasure in fools; fulfill your vow. It is better not to make a vow than to make one and not fulfill it. Do not let your mouth lead you into sin. And do not protest to the temple messenger, 'My vow was a mistake.' Why should God be angry at what you say and destroy the work of your hands? Much dreaming and many words are meaningless. Therefore, fear God. If you see the poor oppressed in a district, and justice and rights denied, do not be surprised at such things; for one official is eyed by a higher one, and over them both are others higher still" (Ecclesiastes 5:4-8).

Wedding vows are essentially promises that you make to one another, and they set the tone for your future together. God says that marriage vows emphasize the importance of a committed, loving, and faithful partnership between a husband and wife. God always keeps His covenant promises, but He can do nothing for us if we do not keep ours. "You shall not swear falsely, but shall perform to the Lord what you have sworn" (Matthew 5:33). "Do not swear at all. Let your Yes be yes and your No be no; anything beyond this comes from the evil one."

Marriage vows are sacred promises. I viewed my wedding vows as fundamental commitments that bind two individuals in a lifelong relationship, emphasizing love, loyalty, and trust.

We had life challenges, such as infidelity and unexpected circumstances, which can test the commitment represented by our wedding vows. I tried to recount my personal experiences of betrayal and struggle, highlighting the emotional turmoil and difficulty in maintaining love and trust after infidelity. Through recommitment and counseling, we took a journey toward healing our marriage involved multiple things.

Through spiritual accountability, I discussed the spiritual implications of breaking vows, viewing them as sacred commitments made before God, with consequences for failing to uphold them. Dealing with the impact of spiritual counseling helped us to document how faith-based counseling helped us navigate our emotional pain and fostered forgiveness and understanding between us.

"Vows are just ceremonial; shouldn't love be enough?" That's a question I'm sure most of those who promote and support marriage get from time to time. I understand the perspective. Love is indeed a powerful and essential component of any relationship. However, marriage vows serve a unique purpose beyond the ceremonial aspect. They are a formal declaration of commitment, trust, and mutual respect between partners. Vows can provide a sense of security and accountability, reminding both individuals of their promises to each other, especially during challenging times. While love is the foundation of a strong relationship, vows can reinforce the commitment to work through difficulties and maintain the bond. They symbolize the dedication to nurturing the relationship and supporting each other through life's ups and downs. Ultimately, the importance of vows can vary from couple to couple, and what matters most is mutual understanding and agreement on how to navigate the relationship together. If love and mutual respect are enough for both partners, that's what truly matters. You want to put in the work to keep your marriage strong, not keep divorce in the back pocket.

Divorce is a personal right if you wish to end your marriage. The reasons for seeking a divorce can vary widely and are deeply personal. Some common reasons include irreconcilable differences, infidelity, financial issues, lack of communication, and emotional or physical abuse. Divorce can be a complex and emotionally challenging process. The marriage vows say, "Two become one." When you divorce, you are literally separating everything you are from the person you married. It is like ripping the seam to make one garment two or more pieces. There is a lot of pain, emotions, and brokenness in divorce. You need to be sure to have support, not judgment, from friends, family, or professional counselors, who can help you walk through that difficult choice.

Forgiveness is key in marriage, but it doesn't require staying married. Forgiveness is about letting go of resentment and anger, and it can be achieved independently of the decision to remain in the relationship. It is a process that allows you to heal and move forward, whether you choose to stay married or not. Forgiveness can help you find peace and closure, or at least enough understanding to not wish or seek to harm others. I hope this will help you. You can decide to leave or stay, but whatever you choose, you have to show grace to yourself and grace to your spouse. Remember, it was not just the two of you who joined together; families did, friendships did, and if you are parents, the emotional well-being of your children is something you have to think about.

# CHAPTER 3

## What My Parents and Grandparents Taught Me About Marriage

"Train up a child in the way he should go: and when he is old, he will not depart from it." (Proverbs 22:6, KJV)

When I think about what I know about marriage, I can tell you straight— my sisters and I learned by watching. My parents and grandparents didn't sit us down and lecture us. They lived their marriage right in front of us.

I didn't see them fight or argue aloud. If they had disagreements, they went behind closed doors. They never let us girls see them disrespect each other. What I did see was that they prayed. They prayed about everything. Prayer was how they handled struggles. Prayer gave them comfort when things got tough. That's what I learned when I got married: You have to pray your way through some things.

One moment I will never forget was when my mama was diagnosed with cervical cancer. My sisters and I were heartbroken, but Mama stood strong. During the battle, she reassured herself and her family with scripture. She would declare Matthew 5:45: "That ye may be the children of your Father which is in heaven: for he maketh his sun to rise on the evil and on the good, and sendeth rain on the just and on the unjust."

She also reminded us of what the Bible says in 1 Corinthians 10:13: "There hath no temptation taken you but such as is common to man: but God is faithful, who will not suffer you to be tempted above that ye are able; but will with the temptation also make a way to escape, that ye may be able to bear it."

She trusted God. One Sunday, she went to the altar and prayed, and after that, she never mentioned cancer again. She put it in God's hands.

My parents taught us about enduring love by showing us. They lived what they wanted us to learn. They taught us that love isn't just about how you feel. Love is about the choices you make, how you act, and how you treat your spouse. They always reminded us that once you're married, it's not just about you anymore. You have to care for your spouse's heart, too. You have to learn to love yourself first, the way God made you, so that you can love someone else right. They showed us how to forgive, not to be selfish, to speak kindly, and to appreciate each other. They never held grudges. They would say pleasant things to each other, give a hug or a kiss, and sometimes bring home a little gift to show appreciation.

I remember Mama would hum gospel hymns when she was upset. Without realizing it, I do the same thing now. She taught me to pray when things didn't feel right. Instead of holding things in, I pray and leave it with God.

My grandmother played a huge role in shaping me, too. My granddaddy passed away when I was about five years old, and shortly after that, we moved to California. I don't have many memories of my grandfather, but my grandmother became a constant in my life. She moved to California in 1964 after her own mother passed away. We were inseparable. Some folks even thought she was my mother because of how close we were.

Late at night, we would sit up talking and laughing, and around midnight, we'd end up in the kitchen. My grandmother would make homemade biscuits, and we would have syrup and scalloped potatoes with onions. Those nights gave me some of my fondest memories. But they were also where I learned some of my greatest lessons about life, marriage, and faith.

She taught me the importance of kindness, forgiveness, and treating others how I wanted to be treated, just like Matthew 7:12 says: "Therefore all things whatsoever ye would that men should do to you, do ye even so to them." And like Luke 6:31, which says: "And as ye would that men should do to you, do ye also to them likewise."

I carried those lessons into my own marriage. When things would go left, I would get down on my knees and pray, just like Mama and Grandma taught me. That's how I made it through hard days. When I couldn't even find the words, I'd hum, just like Mama used to. Prayer always gave me peace.

Forgiveness was another thing we learned from watching our parents. After praying, you had to change your thoughts toward the person who hurt you. You had to check your feelings, your behavior, and your attitude. Holding on to bad feelings only makes things worse. I was taught that Jesus forgave the men who put Him on the cross. In Luke 23:34, Jesus said: "Father, forgive them; for they know not what they do." If He could forgive them, who am I not to forgive?

First Corinthians 13:5 teaches us about real love: "Charity doth not behave itself unseemly, seeketh not her own, is not easily provoked, thinketh no evil." That's unselfish love. That's the love I try to live in my marriage.

The greatest legacy I can leave to my children, grandchildren, and great-grandchildren is my faith. We gave our children back to God as soon as they were born. We raised them in church, taught them the Word of God, and taught them to serve. All my children are active in the church, but I still pray that they fully surrender their hearts to God, just like they were taught. Proverbs 13:22 tells us: "A good man leaveth an inheritance to his children's children." And that inheritance isn't always money. My parents believed that faith and the love of God were the most important legacies you could pass down.

My parents were spiritually united. The life they lived in front of us girls taught us how to love God and one another. My parents believed it was their responsibility to take us to church, not just send us. Both my parents were leaders in the church. My Daddy served as a deacon and Sunday school superintendent. My Mama was a deaconess, a Sunday school teacher, and a choir member. When other members couldn't clean the church, Daddy would volunteer us girls to do it. Through their example, all three of us sisters gave our hearts to the Lord. My oldest sister is now a minister. I used to sing in the choir and worked as a church secretary. Now, I serve in member services. My youngest sister is still a member of the church and is becoming more involved. I thank God for the example my parents set for us.

I gave my life to the Lord in 1979. Our daughter wasn't even one year old at the time. I became a member of the Los Angeles First Church of God under the leadership of Bishop Dr. Benjamin Reid. My faith has helped me deal with many things in my marriage. I watched my parents respect each other's differences and lean on God. Their faith taught me how to work things out and avoid confusion in my own house. I learned that when you trust God, He gives you the wisdom to handle your home.

Back then, we didn't hear much about generational curses or mental health. If anything went wrong because someone was cutting up or acting strange, my daddy would say, "They're crazy. Don't listen to them." But we prayed through everything. Their lives were the testimony. Hebrews 13:4 says: "Marriage is honourable in all, and the bed undefiled: but whoremongers and adulterers God will judge." They honored their marriage and honored God. Their marriage was a model for my siblings and me.

Now, generational patterns and mental health challenges definitely affect marriage today. You see people waiting longer to get married, or many couples choosing to live together rather than marry. But the Bible is still clear about how God views this. 1 Corinthians 7:9 says: "But if they cannot contain, let them marry: for it is better to marry than to burn." 1 Corinthians 6:18 says: "Flee fornication. Every sin that a man doeth is without the body; but he that committeth fornication sinneth against his own body." And 1 Thessalonians 4:3-4 tells us: "For this is the will of God, even your sanctification, that ye should abstain from fornication: that every one of you should know how to possess his vessel in sanctification and honour."

Mama used to tell us plainly, "If you get pregnant before marriage, you will not stay in my house." And we believed her. Ecclesiastes 12:13 says: "Let us hear the conclusion of the whole matter: Fear God, and keep his commandments: for this is the whole duty of man." She feared God, and she raised us to do the same.

My youngest sister was the one who tested Mama the most. She got pregnant and even moved in with her boyfriend. She claimed they were married, but Mama didn't believe it. Mama insisted that they have a church wedding because she wouldn't accept anything else. I never tested my Mama. I respected and feared her enough to know she meant exactly what she said.

Romans 6:12-23 teaches us clearly: "Let not sin therefore reign in your mortal body, that ye should obey it in the lusts thereof... For the wages of sin are death; but the gift of God is eternal life through Jesus Christ our Lord."

Mama taught us that God created marriage between a man and a woman. She didn't care what the world said. Genesis 2:24 says: "Therefore shall a man leave his father and his mother, and shall cleave unto his wife: and they shall be one flesh." That was God's design, and that's what Mama stood on.

Family traditions are important for connecting to your roots, but you also have to balance traditions with today's realities. Some things may need adjusting, but the core values of family, love, respect, and faith should never change. Even though times have changed, the foundation my parents laid is still strong. Today, many young people are living together instead of marrying. Some think marriage doesn't matter anymore. But I know what the Bible says, and I stand on that truth. God's Word hasn't changed.

My parents lived by God's Word. They didn't just quote it—they applied it to how they lived, loved, and raised their family. Looking back now, I know that everything they taught us about marriage was based on prayer, forgiveness, sacrifice, and standing on God's Word. That's the same foundation I've carried into my own marriage and my own family. Their marriage was their testimony. And today, I thank God every day for the legacy they left us.

# CHAPTER 4

# Who Can Find a Good Man - My Father

**M**Y FATHER INFLUENCED MY EXPECTATIONS of men by showing his girls how a man should treat his family. "It is God, then family," my dad would say. "A man should open the door for his date or wife and take loving care of his family. It does not matter how many jobs you have; your family comes first. You put God first, and everything else will fall into place." My dad's standards were exceedingly high, so I expected the men that I dated to be the same.

Dad made sure the bills were paid (all of them) and on time. He would give my mom the money, and she would deposit it in the bank and write checks for the bills. Dad did not buy us what we wanted all the time, but what we needed. My mom did not want for anything. My father did all he could to make my mom happy.

My dad illustrated by showing us what a father or husband should do for his wife and family. My dad would wash the clothes, wash the dishes, comb our hair, cook, and give us a bath when we were little. He would play games with us, and some of the children in the neighborhood would knock on the door for my dad to come out and play with them. He would take us to church, not drop us off and leave. If we had an event to attend, both of my parents were there to cheer us on.

My dad said the way he treated my mom is the way every husband should treat his wife. He also told us not to settle for less. Whatever my mom asked for, he gave or got it for her. My dad always had a job, sometimes three, to make sure we had whatever we needed. My dad showed his love for my mom, and even on his deathbed, he told me, "Make sure you take loving care of your mother."

The qualities my dad modeled that I most admired were his protection of his family. I remembered one Christmas when we went to Lakewood Mall and Del Amo Mall to shop for Christmas gifts. Our car was on its last leg; we had a ragtop convertible car with a hole in the back window, and it was raining. Mom spent over $1,000 on everything we asked for that day. Before my parents died, we laughed about the shape that car was in, and the fact that we should have taken that Christmas shopping money and put the car in the shop to be repaired.

My parents, especially Dad, made sure we knew right from wrong. We would hear Proverbs 22:6, "Train up a child in the way he should go; even when he is old, he will not leave from it," often. And we also knew Proverbs 13:24 well, "Whoever spares the rod hates his son, but he who loves him is diligent to discipline him." Every now and then, my mom would say, "Children, obey your parents in the Lord, for this is right" (Ephesians 6:1); and "Honor thy mother and father, that thy days may be long upon the face of this Earth" (Exodus 20:12). We heard this when she had told us to do something twice and it was getting on her nerves.

Faith played a significant role in my father's life. He made the right decisions, and if he did not, he was man enough to admit it and say, "I was wrong, and I am sorry." While my father was still working, he would read his bible at the dining room table. You could ask my dad any questions about the Bible, and he always had an answer for you. He would tell you where to find it in the Bible and always wrote down the scriptures to back his answers. My children will tell you, "Granddad came out of the womb quoting scriptures."

My dad treated my husband with respect after he got to know him and understand him, even when he did not like the changes he was taking me through. He would say, "Boni, he needs to get it together. I do not want him over to the house if he cannot abide by my rules. I will not stand for it. If you and the kids want to come and stay here, you are more than welcome." My dad also stood up for my husband; he would not allow my brothers-in-law to talk about him.

My dad never intervened or counseled us during our marital trials; however, that never stopped my mother. My dad said my husband had potential. "If he puts his hands on you, then I will step in."

I have to tell you about the time my husband took the car and disappeared. My dad and I went to the police station, and he told the officer, "I am trying to stay out of what is going on between my daughter and her husband, but you need to find him before I do and get my daughter's car back." My dad laid his gun on the counter and said, "I really am serious."

The police officer said, "Sir, we will handle it. Please put your gun down."

The next day, my car was at my parents' home. The kids and I stayed there for about a week.

My feelings for my father made me love him more, and our relationship became stronger. He was still my superhero because whenever we needed him, not just me but us girls, whatever he did for one, he did for us all. My dad would always get it or come when he was called. This went on even after we were married. I always depended on my dad.

He would say, "Where is your husband?"

I would say, "I don't know, so I am calling my daddy," and he would come to my rescue. Husband or not, I always called on my dad.

It is funny, but I can see so many of my father's traits in my husband. I call my husband Lee, which is my father's middle name. My husband does what he can to make sure his family is well taken care of. He is a deacon and head of parking lot security. He is the one who opens the church on Sunday and makes sure the rooms are ready for people to come in. He gets the pastor's breakfast for him and anything else the pastor needs. We have family dinners on Sunday, and my husband cooks. He does household chores without complaining or asking why I haven't done them. I see my dad all in him.

My husband was remarkably close to my dad. He said when my dad died, a part of him died as well.

Fathers absolutely shape their daughters' views of men. Some would agree with that, while others would disagree. My dad set the view for my husband. Even though I did not really fall for a man in the church, I had expectations for my husband. I knew how I wanted to be loved and treated. I saw how my dad treated my mom. My dad was my first major male influence in my life, other than my uncles.

I remember when my now-husband asked my parents for my hand in marriage. He asked my mother first. I am sorry, but I was eavesdropping and being nosy.

My mother said, "Just what are your intentions with my daughter? You need to take loving care of her or leave her where she is. I could tell you no, but she is grown, and I do not want her to run out and elope without our approval. You need to speak with her dad as well and ask him for his approval."

My husband said, "I am going to speak with him as well."

My dad was on the front porch bouncing a golf ball. Once again, I was being nosy and eavesdropping on the conversation. Mind you, my dad never stopped bouncing the golf ball.

My dad said, "Do you love her?"

My husband said, "Yes, I do, sir."

My dad then asked him, "What are your intentions with her? How will you treat her? How will you take care of her?"

My husband said, "My intentions are to love her and take care of her."

My dad asked, "How do you plan on doing that?"

My husband replied, "Do what I can to make her happy. I do have a job, and if need be, I will get another job to make sure her wants are met."

My dad said, "If you cannot keep her happy, then just leave her here with her mom and me. I'm not having you put your hands on her or mistreat her. She will be your wife, not your slave."

My husband said, "Mr. Parker, I am going to do all I can to keep your daughter happy. I am not going to put my hands on her."

My dad said, "Then you have my blessing. What did her mother say?"

My husband answered, "She told me to speak with you, and that is why I came outside to get your blessing. Thank you, Mr. Parker."

"You can call me Dad."

My husband went back into the house and told my mom what my dad had said.

My mom told my husband, "I am passing the torch on to you. Do not let me down. I do not want my child calling us, saying, 'Come get me,' because you did something to her. I promise you, you won't do it again. If you have her dad's blessing, then you have mine as well. I almost did not recognize you; you got your hair cut."

"Mrs. Parker, I have been busy, and I wanted to look right on this day."

By that time, my grandmother had made it to the kitchen and said, "Excuse me, sir, I am Dear."

My husband turned around and said, "I am Darnell. You do not recognize me, Dear?"

"Boy, you cut your hair, you look handsome."

Mind you, I'm still in the living room, moving from chair to couch so I can hear everything that is being said.

My grandmother told my mom, "That boy has potential."

My mom said, "He just asked for Boni's hand in marriage."

My grandmother said, "He is a nice young man. I like him. He is always smiling and taking my bags from me and bringing them into the house."

My dad and grandmother liked my husband more than my mom did. My mom did tell my husband to send an invitation to his parents.

The reason some men cannot lead in godly ways anymore is that some are not taught how to as children. Other men just do not want to. My husband said he loved me, but over the years, he had to learn how to love me. He was in love with the streets, and he knew how to love the streets. Some men lack knowledge and confidence because they had no example of how to lead in a godly way while growing up. My husband learned by watching my dad.

# CHAPTER 5

## Experiencing Relationships Before I Met My Husband

I WAS ENGAGED TO SOMEONE ELSE before I met my husband, Darnell. I called off that wedding because his actions spoke loudly. And I didn't like what they had to say. He didn't want to do anything (and I do mean anything) but hang out with his friends.

The youth department at church (Compton First Church of God) was asked to write to young men who went into the service and were in basic training/boot camp. I was chosen to write for our group, which included my younger sister, Kathy, Larry (Ray's brother), and me. I began writing to Ray, and we developed feelings for each other. We started to date and eventually got engaged. We never really had any time alone, just the two of us. Whenever we would go out, it was either Kathy, Larry, Scrappy (Kathy's boyfriend), or just Kathy, Larry, and me. We would have the most amazing times! Wherever they wanted to go, I would take them and pay for everything. The fun would start on Friday night and end on Sunday night.

My fiancé, Ray, and I could not get it together. The icing on the sour cake was when the four of us went to see The Commodores. Ray didn't want to ride with the rest of the group; he wanted to drive to the show alone, which he did. He ended up getting a parking ticket. He was angry about it and was taking it out on all of us. It seemed we would disagree about any and everything. He was supposed to go and pick out the tuxedo for him and the young men. I kept asking him when he was going to go.

His reply was, "Even if I'm dressed in purple, as long as I am there, it does not matter."

I felt as if things were going downhill. He wanted to spend more time with his friends than with me, so I decided to give him his freedom and called off the wedding.

Shortly after the wedding was called off, I went to see Steven, an old friend. He called himself giving me some advice during a long talk over lunch. I had a wonderful time with him, and he asked me to get back together. I said it would be nice, but I just wanted to be friends. He said it did not hurt to ask. He lived in Aliso Village off 1st Street in LA, and we met a couple of times after that. We went out to Long Beach Pier with Kathy and Larry, enjoyed a nice walk on Redondo Beach, and had dinner.

Steven was a very handsome bi-racial young man; his mom was Caucasian, and his father was Black. He had a nice complexion and long, wavy hair, which he kept in an afro. We called him Jesus Christ Superstar when he let his hair down!

Following our evening, I gave Larry, who lived with Ray, a ride home. On my way home, on the freeway, I was listening loudly to The Emotions' song, "You Got The Best Of My Love." I noticed that someone was following me. Apparently, he could hear the music playing, and he yelled out the window, after he pulled up next to me, that he liked the song. This random man kept following me. He followed me all the way home. Rather than tell him to get lost, we talked briefly, and he asked for my number. I only went out with him once. I don't remember his name, but I remember that both times I saw him, he was wearing white socks! When I got back home from the date, Kathy and Larry were sitting in the living room, throwing white socks back and forth and making jokes. He paid for everything on our date, but he still had to go!

Dating gives you the opportunity to learn more about each other. You ask questions to find out that person's interests, goals, likes or dislikes, and their values, if they have any. You find out whether they put God first, how they communicate, and how they handle conflict. You find out whether they want children and whether they make enough for you to be a stay-at-home mom. Dating can provide a solid foundation for a lifetime relationship with this person.

While dating, I intended to marry that person until I opened my eyes and saw too many red flags. I learned both positive and negative values, and I also found out some personal things while dating. I learned what my strengths and weaknesses were. This helped me see what I need and deserve in a great relationship. The last relationship I had before I got married had a lot of red flags. I stopped and started questioning why I had put up with it for so long. So, after that relationship ended, I learned to avoid unhealthy relationships going forward.

Before I got married, my values were being compromised. After that relationship with Ray, I learned to value the following: respect, trust, and communication are the keys. Being open and honest, listening to your partner, showing appreciation, and practicing forgiveness. I was doing all that; my partner just was not.

First of all, you must know what boundaries mean to set them. Sometimes it is hard to maintain your boundaries out of fear of losing your partner. I figured my feelings—physically and emotionally—should come first. In my past relationship, his feelings and what he wanted to do came first. I was tired of being drained in my past relationship. I was direct, but I kept calm and was very polite until I could not take it anymore. He cared more about his feelings than mine. I did all I could to make it work. When that did not work, I called off the wedding.

I became engaged to Ray, but Steven and I remained good friends. He was my go-to guy whenever I had a problem with my relationships. Steven and I dated for about three years before Ray. After Ray and I became engaged, the relationship went downhill. When I was having problems with Ray, I would call Steven, and we would have long talks out on the beach. His talks with me would help me a lot. Then, problems with Ray would start all over again.

Friends wanted to know why I did not stay with Steven. God had other plans for me, and that's why I did not marry Ray. Shortly after I called off my wedding, I met my husband. I could not let the past make me compare my husband to Ray; they were nothing alike. I was starting all over again with a new person.

When I first started dating (in general), faith was the furthest thing from my mind. I was not saved, and I was not thinking about being saved. I just wanted to date. I knew how I was brought up; being brought up in the church does not make you a Christian. I was not thinking about faith at that time in my life. In the back of my mind, I knew that I could not do certain things or go to certain places, and I definitely could not let my parents find out that I did. I did not give my heart to the Lord until after I got married.

Unlike with Ray, when I started dating my husband, we agreed to have open communication, discuss our finances, and consult with each other before making a large purchase. We talked about our needs and desires. We discussed how I would take care of the inside of the house, and he would take care of the outside, but he sometimes does both. He even cooks and does the laundry. My husband did not want me to work when we got married, but that was one thing we could not compromise on. I enjoyed working, and besides, I was bringing home more than he was.

I overlooked or ignored any warning signs that might have indicated problems, such as his being overprotective or jealous. I found out later that the reason he was overprotective of me was that a former girlfriend named Denise had died in his arms, so he would always look out for me. We would argue: if I wanted to go to certain places, he would suggest

I go with someone, or he would say, "I really would like it if you did not go or attend." Certain places he would go, and he would go there alone because he said he did not want anything to happen to me. This made me feel good because he was looking out for me, but at the same time, I did not like it. I was going all over the place alone before I met him. We barely went anywhere together for fear that something would happen to me.

A challenge for me, early on and over the years, in my relationship with Darnell was the way he spoke to women. It was: "How are you doing, Miss Lady?" or "How are you doing, Sweetheart?" I did not like hearing him speak to another woman like that, but working in the store, that was the way he talked to keep them coming back.

I have really learned a lot about relationships and marriage. I have learned valuable lessons and built a foundation for a successful future. I learned to be patient and wait for the outcome. Marriage builds resilience. God helped me with my experiences, both positive and negative. I became more grounded. God took the bad and made it good. My grandmother was right. When I had fears, challenges, or uncertainty over the years after I started dating and eventually married my husband, she would always tell me to have faith, patience, and trust in God; that I would build up more faith and trust in Him because He would never let me down.

My grandmother was a spiritual mentor to me. She gave me great advice. Then I had my parents, who were always open about how they thought and what I should consider. They would often say,

"Do not move fast, take your time, and listen to your heart." They reminded me of that after I called off the first wedding. "There are plenty of fish in the sea. Go out and get yourself a new wardrobe and start fresh."

You know, dating is one way to build experience; it will help you learn about yourself and others. You are being exposed to different people and their personalities. You will learn what you like and dislike in a person through dating. Communicating with your date helps you become more self-aware. Some people do not know how to hold a conversation or be social. While dating around, you will learn how to bounce back from challenging situations. Dating helps you to see what you really want in a partner. You learn when to talk and when to listen.

On my first date with my husband, he fell asleep during the movie. On the way to my house, he asked if we could stop by a hotel.

My reply was, "For what?"

He said, "So we can talk."

I said, "We can talk while in the car, or we could have held a really friendly conversation at the movies, but you went to sleep. Please take me home."

Heartbreak may be necessary to appreciate love, but it still hurts. You can learn valuable lessons, good and bad. This way, you will appreciate, trust, communicate, and be honest and trustworthy in your relationship. In the wake of heartbreak, you begin to examine yourself to see if it was your fault. After a heartbreak, you become resilient; some people also build up a wall. Some people do not bounce back from a breakup; they are not able to cope with their emotions and mental stability. Heartbreak is not limited to romantic relationships. I have experienced heartbreak in relationships, even in my marriage. It has made me a wiser, stronger, and better person.

God put my husband in my life for a reason, and I am glad He did. My husband has become my best friend, my partner in crime.

# CHAPTER 6

## How I Met My Husband

IN SEPTEMBER OF 1977, WE started attending the Vermont Church of God. Kathy, Larry, and I would walk to Tiger Liquor Store, which was about three doors down from the church, and that is where I met Darnell Reynolds.

Darnell was a smooth-talking, handsome young man. I was buying some candy and gave him a 50-dollar bill. I put out my hand to receive my change, and he touched my hand in a really funny way, smiled, and asked how I was doing. I knew he was a smooth talker and a flirt. I wasn't falling for it.

I told him to put my money on the counter, and I would pick it up. My first impression was that I did not like him. I could not stand being in the same room as him. But if I wanted some candy, I would have to stop before I got to church. He was too smooth for me. I just did not like him.

Once I got to really know him, things began to change. At the end of October, we started dating. I found out Darnell and Rex, his boss, had a $5.00 bet going! Rex told Darnell that the next female who came through the door, he had thirty days to "hit it." Hit it meant to have sex with her. I was the first female to walk through the door after that bet.

Darnell told Rex, "You know that girl does not like me."

Rex told Darnell, "You can pay me now."

Darnell said, "I'll get to know her because I'm not paying you anything!"

This is how our courtship began. We would go to the store on Wednesday nights and Sundays. The next time I went into the store, he started up a conversation with me. I did not know he started talking to me because of a bet. I found out later. Anyway, one thing led to another, and he asked me out on a date.

Darnell and I had been talking for about two weeks when, one Saturday, I came into the store and he gave me $200.00. He would then give me $200.00 every week up until we got engaged.

We went out to dinner one Saturday night, and to my surprise, two of Darnell's brothers came with us: Daryl and Edward. I was so mad with Darnell! Whatever we started to talk about, they both took over the conversation. I was kicking Darnell under the table.

He asked me, "What movie do you want to see?"

Before I could say anything, his brothers took over the conversation.

I said, "Take me home, and y'all can go to the movie together."

One of the things that was a big challenge before we got married was that he sometimes worked at night, which made it hard for us to go out together. I stopped letting my youngest sister use my car and let Darnell use it. My sister was mad. I told her she would get over it. I was always picked up on time or before time, and if he could not get off work, one of his brothers would come and get me, and they would be on time.

Once, while we were at his house, Darnell began singing "Song for You" by the Temptations. His dad said he was singing to him. Now, part of the lyrics says, "*There's no one more important to me (baby). Baby, can't you please see through me 'cause we're alone now and I'm singin' this song for you.*" Those lyrics are not sung to your father, still, his dad and I argued over who Darnell was really singing to.

Darnell did not want to take sides, so he said, "I was just singing."

Darnell asked me to marry him twice, but I kept making excuses not to accept his proposal. He said, "Let's move in together." I told him my parents would not go for that.

Darnell and I went out on a Saturday after that second proposal, and I did not hear from him for a whole week afterwards. I called his house several times, but there was no Darnell. Finally, I said, "Whatever! I have a life, and I am not waiting on him."

I called old faithful Steve, and we agreed to get together that Sunday evening, but around 2:00 p.m., Darnell called. I asked him what he wanted.

He said, "I must see you, and we need to talk. I will be there in less than 30 minutes."

I told Kathy and Larry that Darnell was on his way. Kathy was so mad. She said, "I hate that liquor store boy."

I had already made up my mind that if he was not there in 30 minutes, we were done! He was there within 15 minutes. I called Steve and canceled our evening with him, Kathy, and Larry.

When Darnell got out of the car, I met him at the door. I asked him what was up. He asked me to come outside on the porch. I sat down on the porch waiting for a lie. He said that he was trying to figure things out. He knew he wanted to be with me after being away. I told him he had a funny way of showing it. This was the last of November.

He said, "Will you marry me?"

I said, "Why?"

"Because I love you and I do not want to be without you."

After explaining his reasons, I said yes that time.

With the help of Nita, Mom, and my cousin Georgia, we pulled off a wedding. My cousin Harvey baked our wedding cake. My dress came from Windsor in the Lakewood Mall. I had some friends and family who approved and some who disapproved. The only people who disapproved were my youngest sister and her boyfriend at the time. Not only did they disapprove, but they also hated him.

My play brother told me, "If you like him, go for it." I had called off my engagement with his brother.

My friends were okay with him as long as I was happy. My parents were okay with him. My grandmother liked him a lot.

I was asked if there were any red flags. My answer was no! There were no red flags until we were married. I really enjoyed dating him. But when did I know it was love? Well, after getting engaged, I promised myself that this would be my only marriage. It was the little things that Darnell did that made me fall in love with him. When we went out to dinner, he paid for both our meals. I was not used to that; before, I paid for everything. He would open the door for me. He would often serenade me. Oh, how I loved his voice!

Once, while at his house, I fell ill. He called my parents, and my mom answered. He told her I was going to spend the night because I was not feeling well. She told him to bring me home, and she did not care how. He would call and check on me to see how I was doing. He even came over to the house to see how I was doing. That really made me feel good.

He was changing my life and my perspective on love. I had never felt that way before. I liked his walk, his eyes, his smile, the way he made me feel inside. Even when we didn't agree, he always made me feel like I'd won. It is weird; we really have nothing in common. When they said opposites attract, they were not wrong. I can really say we are that couple.

So after knowing him for only about 3 months, we were married. We did everything together except look for my wedding dress. He even helped me with our wedding invitations. He spoke with my parents about the reception catering menu. We both picked out the flowers. We agreed on the pastor who would lead the ceremony. We agreed on the photographer; I did not know Darnell knew him. As it turned out, he lived down the street from Darnell, and Brother Lynch attended our church. He asked me to go with him and the guys to pick out their tuxedos. We had a nice time at the place.

Even though I said yes after Darnell's third proposal, I can't honestly say I felt like God was guiding me. I really did not. God knows what is best for me. It was God who brought us together and kept us together. It will soon be 48 years (February 2026). There is no way I would be with him; I did not even like him when we first met. Once we began dating, I can honestly say I felt peace, clarity, and a sense of relief. Whether I knew it or not, or wanted to admit it, God was guiding and ordering my footsteps.

Darnell asked me to move in with him before we got married. I said no! I could hear my parents saying, "Why buy the cow when you can get the milk for free?" Then they would say, "Living together before marriage is a sin, just read Hebrews 13:4." Living together is a personal decision that you would have to make. This subject is a toss-up: some people are okay with it, while others are against it. Growing up in a Christian home, my parents were against it. They associated living together with premarital sex, and they were against that.

# CHAPTER 7

# When I Said I Do

Our wedding day came. I was excited. I was scared, too. But there we were at the church on the day we would become husband and wife. I was talking to my dad as he walked me down the aisle. I was nervous at first because Darnell had hung up the phone on me that morning. That was the first time he had ever done that. He felt like I was nagging him about what time to be at the church.

I sent him a note saying, "I love you."

In return, he sent me one saying, "I am here, and I love you more."

That made me feel so much better. Especially, since I was praying that I would not fall while walking down the aisle.

My dad knew I felt like that and told me, "I got you." Then he leaned in and whispered, "Make do of this one because I am only walking you down the aisle one time. If you get married again, you are on your own."

As I got closer to Darnell, I felt a sense of relief. I made it without falling. A weight had been lifted off my shoulders. Though he was so high that he was slightly leaning, I was happy when he took my arm from my dad's and then touched my hand.

We were taught that what God has for you is for you. No one can take that away from you at all. I had a strong sense of peace about the choice I made. I cannot say that something spiritual happened to confirm my choice; I did not ask God for a husband. I did not want a husband when Darnell and I met. We did not go through counseling. We should have, we could have, we just did not. I believe it could have helped us. Yet, I also know that whatever happens in life was already ordained by God before I was born. It is up to us to make the right decision to do the right thing. The choice is always yours. My parents could have been praying for us, but I personally was not praying, asking God, or seeking his guidance.

We really had no spiritual state in our relationship. We were both church-going individuals who believed in God but did not have a relationship with God. We understood each other, which made it easier for us to build emotional intimacy and trust. Even though Darnell did not go to church every Sunday because he was working, I still felt safe with him. He protected me, and I was free to be myself. Our spiritual relationship came after we were married.

We are both proof that people can change. I have a husband who has changed his life for good, not looking back or having second thoughts about the violent life he used to lead. With the grace of God, he was able to walk away from that kind of life after several years in our marriage. We moved from Paramount to the Palmdale/Lancaster area, then to Georgia. Darnell was tired of living that kind of life. By then, he had a family and was getting older. He did not have the time to keep up the gang and thug life. He had finally had enough of his old ways. He could not tell his sons the right way if he was not living it.

My husband would fight you in a heartbeat. My aunt gave him the name of "Aims Home Loan to The Rescue." Whenever there was a problem, my family would always call my husband. He would be right there to handle the situation for them.

God's presence was there with us on our wedding day. It began when the minister started praying and reading scripture. The minister prayed that God bestow big blessings upon our union. The wedding ceremony reflected our faith through the scripture reading, prayer, music, and the wording of the vows. As the minister prayed, we knelt. The decorations, the way the ushers welcomed the guests, and the way they seated them were perfect.

Our family and friends showed us love and support and gave us their blessing. When we did our marital vows, we did not exchange rings. I told him I had a ring, but the ring meant nothing; it is what is in your heart that matters. Because we had a traditional church wedding, some of Darnell's family did not come. Jehovah's Witnesses do not enter churches. But I was not going to change locations. At the wedding ceremony, we were waiting for someone to speak up and object. When the minister said, "Is there any here to object? Speak now or forever hold your peace," we exhaled and thanked God that no one did.

God's presence was there when we got into an accident after the wedding. We didn't realize that the person who hit the car was in the wedding procession until Darnell and his brother got out to assess the damage. Darnell realized it was his next-door neighbor.

Darnell asked him if he was going to the reception, and he replied, "Yes."

Darnell told him to follow us. When we reached my sister's home, we exchanged information. What a mighty God we serve. I also know God's presence was there because Michelle kept pulling blocks in her dad's new Cadillac. A block is blocking cars so they cannot enter or get into the wedding party.

I was not sure how many people would show up. I wondered if I would remember the words that the minister said to repeat after him. I saw loved ones that I had not seen in years. I made sure Brother Lynch took great photos, and he did. We sadly lost them when we moved to Georgia.

I prayed that the food would be awesome, and that Darnell would keep some of his clothes on. In each photo, Darnell was losing bits and pieces of his clothing. I hoped everyone enjoyed the food and each other. I prayed for no disagreements and for everything to run smoothly, and everything worked out as I expected.

We did not allow liquor, wine, or beer at the reception. No smoking was allowed in the house either. My sister had a shed in the back that was connected to the garage, and you had to give a code to get your alcoholic drinks and smoke. It was funny because on several occasions, they almost got caught.

I was an emotional roller coaster. I was experiencing joy and anxiety. At the reception, I got a headache. I lay across my sister's waterbed (wrong thing to do). Darnell took me home and returned to the reception. I did not remember taking off my dress. I obviously fell asleep. Darnell woke me up when he came back home.

On February 18, 1978, we were married by Elder Neighbor at Compton First Church of God at 12 noon. My matron of honor was my oldest sister, Anita Carey. My maid of honor was my best friend, Michelle Conerly. My bridesmaids were Arlece Russell, who is my close friend/sister from church, and my youngest sister, Kathy Hamilton. Barbara Dixon, a friend and church member, sang at our wedding.

The morning of the wedding, I told Darnell to make sure he was at the church at 9:00. We were supposed to be there to decorate the cars. My cousin Georgia was my wedding coordinator. She said at noon the doors would be closed, and no one could enter the church, and she meant just that!

I would tell brides today to have the wedding of their choice and not be afraid to delegate tasks to different people they can trust, so that they can help. This way, they will not be overwhelmed. Cherish every moment of your ceremony. Make sure your photographer or videographer captures those precious memories. Make sure you and your husband-to-be talk about every detail of the wedding; you need each other's support. Always support each other and never forget why you fell in love. Always be available for each other. My husband and I still make time for one another. We try to go out to breakfast every Saturday morning.

We can go back and forth on whether a wedding is a formality. I think wedding ceremonies hold a much more profound significance. Your declaration of love, joy, happiness, and commitment lies in celebrating two becoming one. Those two should become one because you have to have one mind about everything in that marriage, from how many children you'll have to how much you want to save or spend. And you especially have to be on the same boat when it comes to faith.

Darnell's family's spiritual beliefs were different than the way I was raised. Second Corinthians 6:14-15 states, "Do not be yoked together with unbelievers. For what do righteousness and wickedness have in common? Or what fellowship can light have with darkness? What harmony is there between Christ and Belial (the devil)? Or what does a believer have in common with an unbeliever?" We are not to be unequally yoked with unbelievers. If you both are sinners, you are equally yoked, no matter what your religious background is. But those different beliefs can create problems, and you should be ready to deal with them openly.

Just because you believe you are marrying your soulmate and life will be easy, well, that is not true. You still have to put faith, effort, and communication into each other. Your marriage is ongoing work and commitment. Even if you marry your so-called soulmate, you still must work at it. Every marriage takes work, communication, and listening. You can agree to disagree. When things start to go haywire, out of control, or dysfunctional, your marriage becomes chaotic, pray. Prayer absolutely works. Everything isn't going to go the way you want. Keep in mind, there are two of you. Even with your soulmate, you will still have trouble; everything won't be easy or smooth sailing all the time. With your soulmate, keep communication open and support each other in your marriage. Also, remember that marriage requires ongoing effort beyond the first attraction.

# CHAPTER 8

## Marriage and Family Begins

THAT NIGHT, AFTER DARNELL RETURNED home from our wedding reception, there was an unexpected knock on the window. It was his brother Daryl. His father, Eugene, and brother, Edward, were in jail. We had to get up and go to Lynwood to try to bond them out. They would not release them, so we went back home. The next morning, we got up and had breakfast.

We did not go on a honeymoon because we both went to work on that Monday. However, we were passionately physically attracted to one another. At the beginning of our marriage, we had a deep connection. I'm not sure how long our honeymoon phase lasted, but I can tell you that after the first 12 years of marriage, we enjoyed a second honeymoon phase.

Darnell was still working at Tiger Liquor Store. I worked at Catalina Outlet in Torrance as an Assistant Manager while I was in school. I worked the early shift, and Darnell worked the afternoon shift. My manager was Linda (not sure of last name now). Darnell and I had been married for about a month when Linda told me my service was no longer needed. This was because I would never lie for her. She needed me to cover for her since she was gone for about five hours, and the head office was calling for her. I told them she left. To save her skin, she told them she was doing inventory and that I hadn't told her they were calling. My husband did not want me to work anyway.

Then I found out that I was pregnant. About three months after that, we found out the house we were living in was being sold, and we had only a week to move out.

Darnell had to go to court in Torrance to testify, so I went with him. His ex-girlfriend, Denise, was shot in the head. They had gone to a party, and he told her to stay inside while he went outside. Denise came outside anyway and began talking to Darnell. Shots rang out, and she was shot right between the eyes. The bullet went in, but the skin closed back up.

Denise kept asking him, "If he was okay."

He finally said, "Yeah, I'm okay."

She held her head back, and the blood began to run down her face. Darnell had to testify at her trial. The bullet that killed Denise was meant for Darnell. At the trial, they were saying that Darnell set Denise up to be killed. That's when I found out my husband had been a Crip under the leadership of Tookie Williams. The Crips were among the most popular and notorious gangs during that time (they say, once a Crip, always a Crip).

While in court, we saw the man who shot Denise. With all of that and losing our place, we turned to my parents for housing.

After we moved in with my parents, we would go to dinner and breakfast at Carroll's in Gardena. I would order two baked potatoes with extra butter and two vanilla malts. I had to have two slices of cornbread, but only the corners. So, two of everything. When we would leave the house at 2:30 in the morning, I would leave a note on my parents' door so they would not think I had gone into labor.

I was picking Darnell up from work one day when I went into the store. I was very pregnant. There was a man in the store following me around.

I looked back at him with attitude, and he said, "We would have had fun doing it, but you wouldn't be carrying anything."

When I looked over at Darnell, he had jumped over the counter with the shotgun in his hand and told me to leave the store. As I was leaving the store, I heard Darnell tell the young man not to come back into the store, or he would kill him for talking to his wife like that. I asked Darnell why he reacted like that.

He said, "Because you are my wife, and he had no reason to say anything to you."

He said he could not live with himself if anything happened to me, like what happened to Denise.

On Mother's Day in 1978, I was still pregnant with Di'Ara. Darnell went and purchased my first pre-Mother's Day gift. I received a white purse and white shoes. It was the same set that I saw at Lee's Shoe Store in Del Amo's Mall in Torrance. He was so happy to become a dad that he wasn't thinking. He left the receipt in the bag. I returned the set to the store the next day, then went to Lee's Shoe Store and purchased the same set, leaving with $175.00 in my new purse. We had a lovely Mother's Day dinner, and he never knew what I did!

One day in October, my back started to feel uncomfortable. I called the doctor and was told to come to the hospital. I told Darnell I had to take a shower first. I went to the hospital, but I was only dilated four centimeters (about 1.57 inches), so they sent me home. I couldn't sleep, so I sat on the toilet all night. Around noon that afternoon, Darnell took me back to Kaiser Hospital in Harbor City.

He had to be at work at 5:00 p.m., so the doctor told him he could go. I had only dilated five centimeters (about 1.97 inches).

The doctor told me that they were going to perform a Cesarean section (C-section). The nurse told me that they needed to have my mother's signature and permission because I was underage.

I corrected her, telling her, "No! I am 22 years old and married!"

By the time my mom arrived, I had called Darnell at work to let him know that they were going to do a C-section. He said he was on his way back. By the time he arrived, I was coming out of surgery with the baby. I looked at Di'Ara, and she began to cry. I told her she was ugly as well!

I caught pneumonia while I was in surgery, so I had to stay in the hospital and was unable to breastfeed. The doctor came into the room and said they had to put tubes down my throat. Darnell could not take it, so he left. My parents, grandmother, and aunt were there. I did not see Darnell for two days. But the women in my family made sure I became well.

My grandmother said, "Eat all your food and do what the doctor tells you."

They brought me broccoli soup. I poured it into the sink, rinsed the sink out, and put the bowl back on the tray like I had eaten all of it. Of course, I left some in the bowl to make it look like I ate it.

The doctor jokingly told us that our baby was a boarder, and she would be discharged. Nothing was wrong with Di'Ara; she was taking up space. I had to stay because of the pneumonia. Darnell would not let anyone hold Di'Ara or drive the car. So, he drove and held the baby at the same time. He took her to my parents' house.

When he walked into the house, Mama said, "Give me my baby."

Darnell said he had an announcement to make. "No one was to say anything to Di'Ara or spank her."

Mama said, "Boy, give me the baby!"

And he did.

I was in the hospital for nine days. After I was discharged from the hospital, Darnell wanted to stop by his job so Rex, John, Raymond, and his other co-workers could see Di'Ara. He came around to the passenger side of the car to get Di'Ara and take her into the store.

When a young lady he knew walked up to the car, she asked, "Darnell, is this your baby?"

"Yes, she is my daughter," he said.

She then said, "Well, since I'm not the mother, can I be the godmother?"

I got out of the car and started to chase her down the street, C-section, and all. I was praying that my sutures did not come loose! Darnell gave Di'Ara to someone and ran after me. He asked me if I was crazy.

I said, "She was about to find out if you had not grabbed me."

Shortly after Di'Ara was born, we moved to 51st and Gramercy. I went to work at Torrance Medical Center, where I worked with Dr. Lam, a surgeon. I was so glad that my six weeks were up. I was getting tired of looking at the four walls. Darnell had been released from the Los Angeles County Jail right around that time. I memorized all the hospital's and jail's phone numbers just in case I needed them. Darnell took a truck driving job with Coors.

Darnell was invited to a party in Inglewood. We took Di'Ara to her Godmother, Lillian Clark's house. Dee would spend the weekend with the Clarks.

Darnell asked me, "Would you like to go with me?"

I said, "Sure."

It felt great to be going out to a party with my husband. Biker girls began to arrive at the party. After being at the party for a while, we heard people arguing.

Darnell said, "Let's go."

He took me home and went back to the party. When he arrived, the police were there and had arrested everyone.

Darnell knew that I loved Patti LaBelle and Luther Vandross, so we went to their concert. Some young ladies were sitting behind us. One of them was so into Luther singing that she took Darnell's hat off his head, and when he turned to see what was going on, she kissed him on his lips. I slapped his face, and when I turned for her, of course, she ran, and he grabbed me. We stayed until the concert was over, but I was still looking for that young lady.

The evening of the 4th of July 1980, Darnell had taken Anita and her sons, Ereyn and Ethan, home first. On the way to take Di'Ara and me home, he informed me that he was going over to a friend's house to unwind. He came into the house to change his clothes. I tried to talk him out of leaving because he had been drinking already. I told Darnell that if he was going out drunk, he could get hurt or hurt someone."

He said, "I'm going anyway."

He had a car full of alcohol and beer. I did not feel right about him leaving. He will tell you that I put a curse on him.

About five hours later, my parents knocked on our door. Darnell had been in an accident and totaled the car. I am not sure which one of them told me that part.

"He had nothing but liquor and beer cans in the car," said my mother. "Get dressed, and we will take you and the baby to the hospital." While I was getting dressed, my mother got Di'Ara dressed and made her a couple of bottles.

When we arrived at the hospital, I signed in to see him, not knowing that his mother was already there. When the nurse called Mrs. Reynolds, his mother and I both got up.

I said, "Excuse me, but I am his wife."

We began arguing over who would go back to see him first. I finally said she could go. When I did go back to see him, his left eye was hanging. The doctor tried to fix it the best he could. I had Darnell transferred to the hospital where I knew he would get the best care, and I stayed with him. My parents took Di'Ara home with them.

On the way to Torrance Memorial Medical Center, I rode in front of the ambulance. I had the paramedics play all the different sounds on the siren. My husband was in pain, but I was having the time of my life.

Once we got there, Dr. Lam took one look at his eye and told Darnell, "I can do a better job."

Doctor Lam wanted me to assist him in surgery. I said, "NO!!!"

I was running out of the electric double doors, so he knew I meant no. But I did not wait for them to open. I hit them with my whole body, and then they opened. Later, I was told that I had broken the doors. I did help Dr. Lam with surgery, and my husband's eye still looks great.

Darnell was discharged from the hospital for having liquor inside his pillowcase. He was having my brother-in-law, Ed Carey, bring him crack into the hospital. He had others to bring things in as well. Three days after he was discharged, he cut his cast off his broken leg. I did not realize it was off until I rolled over, and he said, "Ouch."

I pulled the covers back, and I saw that the cast was off. He had to go back to the hospital to have another cast put on due to the pain.

The doctor gave him a shot and told him, "If you take this one off, don't come back."

He took it off, and he did not go back.

After we left the doctor's office, we went by the liquor store to pick up some cigarettes and beer. On our way into the store, this young man bumped into Darnell. Darnell looked at him, and the young man said, "I will mess you up more than you are already."

Darnell was the wrong person to say that to. Darnell told me to take the bag to the car and get inside. The young man would not come out of the store. He should never have started something he could not finish! Darnell proceeded to go back into the store when I told him, "Let's just go home."

I began working at Prairie Medical Group as the Medical Records Supervisor. I managed over six employees. This job was closer to the house, paid more, and was less stressful.

About three weeks after I got this new job, I found out that I was pregnant again! I asked two of my co-workers, Phyllis, and Monica, to be godmothers. I was being cared for by Dr. Taska, who was one of the best doctors in town. My prenatal checkups were going fine.

On the morning of November 26, 1980, a day before Thanksgiving, we picked out a name for our daughter: Di'Ana LaNae Reynolds. I went into surgery, but I was not put to sleep since it was a C-section.

As Doctor Taska was delivering the baby, he said, "Boni, I don't like her color."

At that point, I was put to sleep. I woke up in the recovery room, and I asked the nurse about my baby, and once again, I was put to sleep. When I woke up for the second time, Darnell was in the recovery room with me. I knew something was wrong because he was there. I began to cry, and so did Darnell.

I was moved to a regular room, and when Darnell walked into the room, I could see the pain in his face. He said, "Di'Ana was holding one of my fingers with a smile on her face. She then closed her eyes and took her last breath. The nurses came and wrote down the time of death."

He would not allow them to take her downstairs to the morgue in a body bag. He carried Di'Ana downstairs in his arms. They took several pictures of her, which we lost in the move to Georgia.

I contacted the insurance company we signed up for approximately 5 months before Di'Ana's birth. We believed it was a great company, but they said we had to be insured for 6 months to be covered! We had to pay for her burial out of pocket. Darnell was so upset. What good is having insurance when you are unable to use it?

I was moved to the third floor of the hospital. Doctor Taska told the nurse to allow as many people to come into the room as I wanted. Both of Di'Ana's godmothers came to see me, as well as my family and friends; Darnell, Mama, and my sister Anita, who left the hospital to plan services at Adams Funeral Home in Compton. Doctor Taska and his associate, Doctor Van, also came to visit me. Both doctors were very apologetic.

I said, "I didn't hold either of you accountable. It is not your fault."

With my faith in God and with all the prayers, love, cards, and phone calls, I was able to sustain us through all that we were going through (Psalm 121:1-2). As I write about my darling little angel, tears fill my eyes. It is still hard to express what took place without crying.

After being discharged from the hospital, I went to Mom and Dad's house until after the funeral. Mom, Di'Ara, and I went to the store at Del Amo Mall to get a dress for Di'Ara and me for the funeral. I had to leave the store and sit in the car. I heard a baby crying and could not handle it. I was an emotional wreck. My husband was so incredible during this time in our lives, but he never expressed his feelings. He was blaming himself for her death.

I had Mom and Nita get the outfit that Di'Ara was christened in. This would be the outfit Di'Ana would be dressed in. Di'Ana's body was laid to rest at Angeles Abby Memorial Park in Compton. The only time I saw my baby was when she was lying in the casket. I am so grateful and blessed to know that our baby is in heaven with Jesus.

We were having dinner one night, and Darnell and I both said at the same time, "Where did that baby come from?" Di'Ana was White with black hair in a pageboy style. My Grandmother said that her color was not going to change. She looked at her nail bed, her feet, and her ears.

Darnell and I were talking as I was writing this chapter, and he said, "It would be nice for us to go to California and visit her grave and place some flowers on it." The tears begin to flow down my face.

We had a graveside service for Di'Ana. I went up to the casket to see her. I wanted to touch, hold, and kiss her. I could not move. I was like a statue. Pastor Reid picked me up by my arms and moved me to the side. One of the songs they sang was "Yes, Jesus Loves Me." Even now, tears come to my eyes when I hear or sing that song.

Every year since Di'Ana's death, my husband says I go into a deep depression and become withdrawn around November 23rd through the 30th. In 2006, we found out that my daughter was going to have a girl. She asked if she could name her daughter after her sister, Di'Ana. I said yes. When our daughter gave birth to my only granddaughter, I held her before her mother and took her out the side door for my husband to hold.

Still mourning, when I went to the doctor for my six-week checkup after the death of Di'Ana, I was told I was pregnant!

I asked the doctor, "How did that happen?"

He laughed and said, "You were there."

I said, "Not really. I don't remember anything. You had given me some medication to take."

Di'Ana's godmother, Monica, who was Dr. Taska's nurse, started calling me "Fertile Myrtle" and telling the patients to talk to me, that I had six children already, and that this time I was having triplets, so nine kids total.

My cousin Jackie and my dad's sister, Aunt Julia, came to see Dad and our family. Jackie and I became close. We decided to take Jackie to Hamburger Henry's in Long Beach. We were walking when two young ladies skated by.

One said, "You can do that to me all day long, and I bet you I will not become like that."

Darnell started laughing. I took off after her. He caught up with us and said she was playing. I said I was not.

Jackie said she did not think it was funny either. We had a wonderful time at Hamburger Henry's. They had over 150 diverse kinds of hamburgers on the menu. Jackie and I had the regular cheeseburger, and Darnell had the cheeseburger with an over-easy egg on top. On the menu, they had peanut butter and jelly, avocado, and bacon burgers, to name a few. We took Jackie back to Mom and Dad's, picked up Di'Ara from Mr. and Mrs. Clark's house, which was across the street from my parents' house, and went home.

During spring 1981, while I was pregnant again, I kept all my appointments with Dr. Taska. He ordered an amniocentesis, and we had to go to a special clinic in downtown Los Angeles to have this procedure done. When the nurse pulled out the needle, Darnell left the room, and the nurse laughed at him. He finally came back into the room and held my hand through the procedure. An amniocentesis is a procedure where fluid is drawn from the amniotic sac. It is done to diagnose chromosomal abnormalities and fetal infections, as well as for sex determination. This test is usually done between 15 and 20 weeks (about 4.5 months) of pregnancy. It takes 10 to 14 days to receive the test results.

They told me to go home and rest because I could have a miscarriage after having the amniocentesis test done. I was told not to lift, climb, walk up hills, and to avoid strenuous exercise and sexual activity for a day or two. As a result of the test, we found out we were having a boy, and everything was okay!

On June 23, 1981, Darnell was arrested for carrying a concealed weapon in the car. It seems as if every time everything is okay, I get hit with something else. *Lord, please give me strength,* I prayed. I began to read Psalms 91:1-2: "He that dwelleth in the secret place of the most High, shall abide under the shadow of the Almighty. I will say of the Lord, He is my refuge and my fortress: my God; in him will I trust." After reading this, I began to sing, "My Faith Looks Up to Thee."

At one of my appointments, Dr. Taska and I talked and scheduled a date for my C-section. It would be on October 8th, 1981. I was expected to be at the hospital no later than 6:00 am to prepare for surgery. Before Darnell went to jail, we decided to name our son after him: Darnell LaMark Reynolds II. I refused to have Junior at the end of my baby's name. I did not want anyone to call him Junior or Little Darnell.

After he was born, several nurses in the hospital asked if I would keep baby Darnell in the room with me.

I asked, "Why?"

They replied, "Because your baby wakes up crying, and his crying wakes up all the other babies in the nursery, then goes back to sleep."

His Auntie Nita gave Darnell II the nickname of Markapu. As he got older, we all started calling him Mark because of his middle name, LaMark. His dad, to this day, only calls him Darnell. When I'm mad, I call him Darnell LaMark. I would hold Mark all the time; I did not want to put him down. Doctor Taska called this filling the void.

Two years after Darnel II was born, I became pregnant with our fourth child. We were living in Paramount. One Saturday night, we went to a church function. It was the Annual Debutante Ball. I wore a cream satin dress that Darnell liked. I was about 2 ½ months pregnant. I was at the function with my parents. The children were at home with my grandmother. They served dinner and were about to announce the winner of the Debutante Ball, which meant whoever raised the most money, when I had to go to the bathroom. To my surprise, I was spotting. I called Doctor Taska's office and spoke with the on-call doctor. I was told that if the spotting continued, I would need to go to the ER.

On Sunday, I was still spotting, so I went to the ER. Doctor Johnson was the on-call doctor, and since I worked with him, I was comfortable seeing him.

He told me, "Since you lost one child, you might as well have an abortion. You're going to lose this child anyway!"

I told him NO! Sometimes women can spot and still have the baby! Since Doctor Johnson spoke to me like that and I worked with him, I could only imagine how he talked to his other patients.

One of my female cousins was over at the house. Darnell was back in jail. I told her my back was extremely uncomfortable. She told me that I was in labor. I had never been in labor, so I did not know what labor felt like. I called Doctor Taska, and he told me to go to the hospital. My cousin drove me to Centinela Hospital in Inglewood. While in the waiting area, I told the clerk I was having more back pain, and she asked how far along I was. I told her three months and two weeks. She said that Dr. Taska was on his way down but that he was called into an emergency C-section. I was in the waiting area for no more than five more minutes when I felt like I had to use the bathroom. I told the clerk, but before she could get me, this child decided she did not want to wait! I was immediately rushed into a room. I had expelled quite a bit in the waiting room.

When Doctor Taska came down, he performed a surgical procedure called dilation and curettage (D&C). I was released, and my cousin took me home. I was not in any pain, but my back was uncomfortable.

The judge sentenced Darnell to prison this time for assault and battery, which is threatening a person with the act of making physical contact with them. The prison was located in Chino, which is near Pomona, California. I'm not sure why he had to rob the person or try to rob the person when he had just gotten paid. This was in 1984.

I was still pregnant with DeOndre' while all of this was taking place. I had to have another amniocentesis done, and my grandmother went with me. Darnell was still at the Los Angeles County Jail waiting to be transferred to Chino. I was told to avoid walking up hills, lifting anything heavy, worrying, stress, jogging, aerobics, douching, exercise, and sex. I was instructed to go home and rest. My doctor had a tight rein on me. Instead of going to the doctor once a month, I was going twice a month.

After working for about another five months, the doctor placed me on complete bed rest. But the kids and I kept going to Chino. The inmates could have a picnic on the grounds with their families, and the kids needed to spend time with him, even there.

This was an emotionally hard time for me, because it was also my responsibility to take my mother back and forth to Kaiser to see her doctor for cancer treatments. After the suggestion of laser surgery on one visit, Mom had to break down and tell Dad about her diagnosis, why she had not told him before, and about the procedure. She knew he would be suspicious if she were not at home, and she would not lie to him. Her coming clean with Dad gave me courage. I finally told Darnell that my doctor had put me on bed rest, and I could not come to see him anymore for a while. The kids and I moved in with Mom and Dad.

After giving birth to DeOndre', I got back on my feet.

CHAPTER 9

# *Why I Stayed Married*

WHAT KEPT ME COMMITTED THROUGH the betrayal of adultery, multiple times, and jail time, numerous times, was the Lord. I had God's grace and glory. In 1 Peter 4:8, "Above all, love each other deeply, because love covers over a multitude of sins." In Matthew 6:14-15, "For if you forgive other people when they sin against you, your Heavenly Father will also forgive you. But if you do not forgive others their sins, your Father will not forgive your sins." Ephesians 4:32: "Be kind and compassionate to one another, forgiving each other, just as in Christ God forgave you."

I loved my husband very much. I also wanted him to pay for what he had done. After I got a call at work one day from a woman who detailed some things about her relationship with my husband that made me madder than mad, I went to our pastor. I told him I wanted a divorce. I told him I wanted to kill him and her. I was at the altar for over a year, asking God to forgive me. When I would leave the altar, I would think of another way to kill him.

I trusted the Lord with all my heart until my husband cheated on me. I had to ask the Lord for forgiveness because Darnell was grown, and he knew right from wrong. He could have said no. I went to the Old Testament, Exodus 21:24: "But if there is serious injury, you are to take life for life, eye for eye, tooth for tooth, hand

63

for hand, foot for foot, burn for burn, wound for wound, bruise for bruise." And Leviticus 24:20: "fracture for fracture, eye for eye, tooth for tooth. The one who has inflicted the injury must suffer the same injury." Deuteronomy 19:21: "Show no pity: life for life, eye for eye, tooth for tooth, hand for hand, foot for foot." I was looking for biblical support to act on my righteous indignation.

I listened to God, but then I followed my angry heart. At that point, I wanted him to feel the pain he caused me and to know just how I was feeling. I wanted him dead. So, I know I was not following my faith at that time. Being in love was not enough. You could be in love, but the other person is not really in love with you. You can be in love and still desire to hurt the one you love. Your actions speak louder than words. None of that is how God designed love for us to live out. That is not patient, kind, charitable, not vain, humble, caring, long-suffering, forgiving, merciful, or gracious. That was me deciding to count the reasons I had to be mad, stay mad, and act out in my madness. For me to be in love with someone, they have to show me the depths of their love for me and respect me. I need to be able to respect and trust them as well. And for me, there can absolutely be no lies. I cannot stand a liar. Cheating meant living in a series of lies.

We had to seek help from a marriage counselor. Our counselor was a tremendous help to our relationship. It was the grace and will of God that we stayed together. It hurts me as I am writing this that I really wanted him dead. *God, please forgive me.* I was not raised that way. Even now, some people try to take my kindness for granted. I had to keep scriptures on love, forgiveness, and kindness to help guide me through the process. Prayer had a significant impact despite the difficulties, opposition, and setbacks. The song "There's a Bright Side Somewhere," fasting, and praying were my weapons. In 1 Thessalonians 5:15-18, we are told, "Make sure that nobody pays back wrong for wrong, but always strive to do what is good for each other and for everyone else. Rejoice always, pray continually, give thanks in all circumstances; for this is God's will for you in Christ Jesus."

Prayer is powerful for perseverance in a marriage. Prayer and faith help you to heal, forgive, love, and restore your marriage. After that year at the altar on my knees, I surrendered it all to Jesus and trusted in God's timing. "I trust in God, I know He cares for me, on mountain bleak or on the stormy sea; Though billows roll, He keeps my soul, My Heavenly Father watches over me."

God worked everything out. But I had to surrender myself totally unto Him. The Lord knows I could not do it on my own. God spoke to me through the scriptures. Psalm 34:17-18: "The righteous cry out, and the Lord hears them; he delivers them from all their troubles. The Lord is close to the brokenhearted and saves those who are crushed in spirit." And Jeremiah 33:3: "Call to me and I will answer you and will tell you great and hidden things that you have not known."

Trials can have a transformative purpose, leading you to patience and completeness. God spoke to me through others, and as I prayed, speaking to God also helped me grow spiritually. God was showing and guiding me with His truth. By reading and meditating on my Bible, I began to see clearly what God was trying to say to me in a still, small voice.

A lot changed after we sought counseling. We began to rekindle the relationship we had when we first met. We grew stronger, we learned to listen to each other more, and we developed honest communication. It became easier to resolve conflicts. Our counselor gave us activities to do between each session. I just completed one of the assignments she gave us. It is more than thirty years later. Our counselor has gone on to be with the Lord.

Our love was able to endure. When we had challenging times, love, persistence, forgiveness, and understanding helped. Love covers a multitude of faults. Also, 1 Corinthians 13 says love is hopeful and believes the best in others. 1 Corinthians 13:7: "Love bears all things, believes all things, hopes all things, endures all things."

Enduring love can and will withstand the testing of time. It is also resilience, forgiveness, and an unwavering commitment to putting God first in our lives. To help our marriage stand the test of time, we have to be dedicated to each other, be respectful, build trust, and spend quality time together; this has helped our relationship endure. Being supported by biblical teachings on love's qualities does not stop once you think everything is going great. Keep reading your Bible and praying that God will continue to keep us together.

I did not set any boundaries until we started seeing the marriage counselor. I even set sexual and emotional boundaries. I was able to express my feelings to him, and he was honest, trustworthy, and respectful. As for my sexual boundaries, I said no a lot. I was able to provide limits in our relationship. I had to put my foot down, and he had to agree to the terms, walk, or I was going to leave.

But if I had left before counseling, and even for a while in counseling, I would not have been coming back. I spoke with our pastor, who asked to speak with both Darnell and me. I still wanted a divorce. I was still tired of the lies, infidelity, and broken trust. Our marriage was no longer beneficial to us; that's what I believed. I did not want him to lead a double life, so I was giving him his freedom. He had to change his lifestyle. I was suffering from mental abuse. I had had it with him. I wanted him to feel the pain I was feeling.

Our pastor asked him if he loved me and told him to tell the truth. He said he loved me. Our pastor told him that if he did not show me how much he loved me, seven times seven (49) devils would come out of me. The pastor said he was telling the truth; I did not believe him.

The difference between enabling and enduring is that enabling involves actions that unintentionally help someone continue harmful behaviors by looking the other way or by ignoring what is happening. Enduring is to tolerate what is going on without putting a stop to the unpleasantness.

I did not want anyone to know just how stupid I was for putting up with his mess for so long. I only spoke with my mother, grandmother, and sisters. My best friends found out about it after I got up the nerve to tell them. My mother's advice was to "go home and talk with your husband. Try to work things out." I did not want to hear what she had to say.

My grandmother said, "Darnell has potential and was not raised like you were." I did not want to hear that either.

My sisters, on the other hand, demanded, "Let's find her, beat her butt, and then get him." My kind of girls. One for all and all for one. We might not always agree, but when we needed one another, we were always there.

While I didn't want to hear my Mom or Grandmom, they were right. If you're considering separation, pray about it first. Think about your well-being, try or consider professional help, and find ways to find each other again. I would ask you if you've actually sat down and talked about the problems. I mean, talked, not yelled, not cursed at each other, but talked to each other civilly. I do not think you should leave at the first sign of trouble, unless that first sign is definitely that you are in an abusive relationship or marriage, or one where addiction, alcoholism, or other dangerous behaviors are normal. Then, leave IMMEDIATELY! Word of wisdom: do not tell your problem to everyone. Some people like to keep the mess going, and they may know more about your mess than they let on.

Some marriages can survive addiction. There is a long list of possible addictions. You have drugs, alcohol, opioids, stimulants, gambling, shopping, food, and sex. Part of a marriage surviving is the addicted person being delivered from their habit. Like I set boundaries with Darnell, you have set limits, you have to be ready to leave if that is necessary, and you have to be clear that they cannot abuse, neglect, or choose things that can lead to death over you. If you are a believer, grace and mercy have to be shown. God shows it to us. While your spouse is recovering, be supportive and help with the healing process. It will take effort from both of you. Please do not go blaming one another. Make sure you stay on your knees before God. He will not give you more than you can bear.

Loving the one you married (or are dating or engaged to) should not hurt you. Your relationship should be built on trust, respect, loyalty, and forgiveness. ***Love should not hurt.*** Your spouse should not put you in a harmful or dangerous situation. If you love someone, you do not want to see them cry or get hurt. By thing has always been, if you love me, you are not going to hurt me or allow someone else to hurt me. Your marriage should not get out of hand while you are talking or disagreeing with one another. You can agree to disagree. It should never escalate into violence, abuse, or even death. You should not have to have the police at your home. When you love someone, you do not talk down to each other, nor do you try to control your spouse.

# CHAPTER 10

# God's Assignment for Marriages Today

THE DIVINE PURPOSE OF MARRIAGE today is to glorify God's covenant and to provide redemption and emotional support. For two individuals to become one also includes financial, sexual, religious, and social commitment to each other. Marriage today is about building a family, raising children in a loving and supportive environment, and fostering spiritual growth as you walk in a deeper relationship with God. Marriage is a covenant between a man and a woman. Marriage should be like Christ's relationship with the church. "It is seen as a sacred bond, a covenant between two individuals intended to reflect a deeper relationship with God."

Love and companionship are the number one priority, always putting God first. And yes, marriages today should reflect Christ, with God being prioritized and kept at the center of your marriage. Build trust and communicate openly and honestly. Make a commitment to lifelong learning and growth in your relationship with God and your faith. Marriage should be a sacred union. A husband and wife should be able to respect each other and resolve their conflicts in a biblical way.

The husband is the head of the house. He is the spiritual leader of the family, as Christ is the head of the church. The husband is the leader; he is not in control or the dominant person in the house. The husband and wife should still submit to one another. Look in Ephesians 5:22: "Wives, submit yourselves to your own husbands as you do to the Lord." Biblically, the husband has the responsibility to lead and to set an example of love, as Christ would have him do.

Couples serve God together by praying together, engaging in Bible study, serving in church together, and supporting each other and others in their spiritual growth. By seeking God's blessing and his guidance for their marriage and for their family. By praying for others, which includes the church, their pastor and his family, the nation, family, friends, the sick and shut-in, and those who are in the hospital and nursing homes. By encouraging each other and holding each other accountable in their faith in God. By putting the needs of others before your own.

Romans 8:28 says, "And we know that for those who love God all things work together for good, for those who are called according to his purpose." Romans 15:5-7 says, "May the God of endurance and encouragement grant you to live in such harmony with one another, in accord with Christ Jesus, that together you may with one voice glorify the God and Father of our Lord Jesus Christ. Therefore, welcome one another as Christ has welcomed you, for the glory of God."

The legacy that marriages leave for their children is, as a spiritual mother, love, faith, and stability. We should leave a legacy to help them understand the love of God and the purpose of their lives. Keep a positive influence going for the next generation. If they are going through difficult times, remind them to read Matthew 6:33: "Seek ye first the kingdom of God and His righteousness and all these things will be added unto you." They will be able to go before the Lord on their own and ask God for wisdom and His understanding to do the right thing. In Philippians 4:13: "I can do all things through Christ who strengthens me."

I see our marriage as a ministry; we support each other as we actively serve our Bible-teaching church. We have to learn how to prioritize the needs of each other's relationships with Christ and our church. We do not just personalize our happiness; we are here to fulfill God's purpose and His love for the world.

My message to couples in a crisis is that there is no single way to answer or help other couples. Seek God's help for the answer, not just your own. You have to have empathy and listen to each other intently, and please do not be judgmental. If they are talking and it becomes heated, take some time out and regroup. Take time out to calm down and gather your thoughts to be helpful. Just know that the crisis will not be resolved immediately or overnight.

Marriage has matured my faith in forgiveness with disagreements and conflicts. I am not selfish and encourage others, as well as myself. We share values and goals. We support each other when we have challenges. I have resilience, hope, and with faith, a better way of doing things.

Forgiveness plays an important role in marital relationships. It helps you move on from past conflicts and misunderstandings; it enables you to build or rebuild trust, and it strengthens the bond between the couple. It also builds longevity and happiness in your relationship. You can lose bitterness and also resentment. Forgiving others helps you to free yourself from the burden that may be holding you down. Also, you need to forgive so Christ can forgive you.

Matthew 6:14-15: "For if you forgive other people when they sin against you, your Heavenly Father will also forgive you. But if you do not forgive others their sins, your Father will not forgive your sins."

Luke 6:37: "Do not judge, and you will not be judged. Do not condemn, and you will not be condemned. Forgive, and you will be forgiven."

It is not good to hold on to negativity, anger, resentment, bitterness, or that unusual desire to want to physically harm someone (like I had). It is not good for your health. Forgiveness helps you heal and build a stronger, more loving relationship with yourself, God, and the one you are committed to.

We should be proud to be ordained and in kingdom marriages. A "Kingdom Marriage" is a biblical relationship in which you and your partner put God first and intentionally practice biblical principles, prioritizing your purpose, support, and spiritual growth to expand God's kingdom. We have to be more like Christ's love for the church. In other words, more like Christ in everything that we do, whether it is at home, church, work, or the store. If you put God first, you will not go wrong. Proverbs 3:6: "In everything you do, put God first, and he will direct you and crown your efforts with success."

Marriage is not only for companionship or sexual fulfillment. I would say that, even though both are important, marriage also involves goals, respect, love, and commitment. Having open communication, covered in prayer, fasting, and studying God's Word are all part of what you need to cook for success.

Yes, you absolutely need God in your life to make your marriage work and last. You will have issues in your marriage, but with God on your side, you have a Masterful Teacher to give you instructions meant just for your relationship. With God in your marriage, you establish a spiritual connection between you and your spouse. With God in your marriage, you will have wisdom and understanding, along with love and unity.

# CHAPTER 11

# If Death Has to Be the End of Marriage

"UNTIL DEATH DO WE PART" means graveyard dead, not love dead. Marriage only ends when we die. It is a commitment for life. "Until death do we part" is part of the wedding vows. For a Christian, the only time you are separated is by death. Romans 7:2: "For example, by law a married woman is bound to her husband as long as he is alive, but if her husband dies, she is released from the law that binds her to him." Also, in 1 Corinthians 7:39, "A woman is bound to her husband as long as he lives. But if her husband dies, she is free to marry anyone she wishes, but he must belong to the Lord."

After 47 years, I cannot imagine life without my spouse. It would be hard to adjust my life without him. I would have a lot of mixed emotions and grief. I would cry a lot because I miss him. I would have to keep myself busy and my mind occupied. I imagine I would be praying to God often and asking, "Why?" I have been told it is one of the most stressful and painful events you can go through in life.

I remember the toll it took on my mom. They had been together since she was 17. My dad was six years older than she was. My dad passed away in his sleep; my mom blamed herself. She said that as a wife, she should have known. My dad passed away in 2019, and my mom in 2023. She passed away in that same room. She had moved all her belongings into that room, which was not their bedroom, and refused to come out. She would sit by the window and watch the cars go by.

As I imagine my mom was, I would be sad, mad, depressed, lost, but relieved that he is no longer in pain. I would be upset because he left me. While I trust God and know that His ways are not our ways, I'm not sure I would be prepared spiritually or emotionally. We are all going to die, but a significant part of your life, the one you have been joined with as one connected being, is gone. In Hebrews 9:27, "And as it is appointed unto men once to die, but after this the judgment."

We do have life insurance and burial plots for each other. Death is just something we do not talk about unless we are at a funeral. I am not prepared; I am still dealing with the death of my parents. I pray that if anything were to happen, God would give me the strength to keep going. I pray for comfort to keep me on the right track.

Dealing with grief, felt as if our marriage was ending. This was in 1980, when our daughter Di'Ana LaNae passed. He became MIA after her death. He blamed himself and said he had to deal with what he needed to alone. Losing a child can affect your marriage in unusual ways. Some people grow closer to each other and find strength in encouraging one another. On the other hand, some experience divorce, resentment, misunderstanding, conflict, and stress while becoming distant from one another. Everybody grieves in unusual ways. Some become withdrawn, isolate themselves, stay out all night, use drugs, drink, etc. The death of a child can lead to feelings of blame, anger, and even separation, but open communication and shared grief can help couples find resilience.

About a month after our daughter's death, we sat down on the couch and began to talk. We shared our grief, and we supported one another mentally and emotionally. I was having a lot of different feelings going on in my body. We found strength and resilience after our long and deep conversation. It helped me a lot.

Yes, Jesus can restore even from death, and I have the scriptures to back it up. Jesus raised Lazarus from the dead, the daughter of Jairus, the son of the widow of Nain, and the son of the Shunammite woman. John 11:41-44: "So they took away the stone. Then Jesus looked up and said, 'Father, I thank you that you have heard me. I knew that you always hear me, but I said this for the benefit of the people standing here, that they may believe that you sent me.' When he had said this, Jesus called in a loud voice, 'Lazarus, come out!' The dead man came out, his hands and feet wrapped with strips of linen, and a cloth around his face. Jesus said to them, 'Take off the grave clothes and let him go.'"

2 Kings 4:32-35: "When Elisha reached the house, there was the boy lying dead on his couch. He went in, shut the door on the two of them, and prayed to the Lord. Then he got on the bed and lay on the boy, mouth to mouth, eyes to eyes, hands to hands. As he stretched himself out on him, the boy's body grew warm. Elisha turned away and walked back and forth in the room and then got on the bed and stretched out on him once more. The boy sneezed seven times and opened his eyes."

The grief that comes with the possibility of divorce felt like death. The end of our marriage could have, and does, signify the end of growing old together or sharing a future. As a wife, I want to leave a positive legacy for my husband. I want to leave my love for him, my desire to cherish and value him, and for him to continue loving God and our family. This is the most important investment I can make. That and to continue telling others about Christ and how He died that we might have everlasting life with Him. Just remember to "Do unto others as you would have them do unto you."

You can grieve and honor your vows because they remain a priority. Your strength and resilience in your marriage are a true testament of your faith in God because He will see you through it all. Grief can be transformed into eventual joy. John 16:20: "Very truly I tell you, you will weep and mourn while the world rejoices. You will grieve, but your grief will turn to joy."

A spiritual bond is eternal for some people, but not for others. Some people, me included, feel that the spiritual bond is until death do you part, or a spiritual awakening where they outgrow each other spiritually. Right now, Darnell and I have an eternal bond, which is our faith in God, who makes our spiritual bond eternal.

When we renewed our vows, we pledged to each other and to God, before the people, a lifetime of devotion and love, that we would be there through thick and thin, through difficulties, to encourage and uplift each other in challenging times. When we faced challenges and situations, we would work it out, and if we could not come to an agreement, we would go before the Lord. Ephesians 5:31: "For this reason a man will leave his father and mother and be united to his wife, and the two will become one flesh." At the end of the day, some marriages support an eternal spiritual bond grounded in faith, with couples pledging lifelong devotion and mutual support through challenges.

I still see my husband as God's assignment to me. What God has joined together, let no man or woman put asunder. He has taken on his responsibility as the head of the household. 1 Corinthians 11:3: "But I want you to understand that the head of every man is Christ, the head of a wife is her husband, and the head of Christ is God." Ephesians 5:25: "Husbands, love your wives, just as Christ loved the church and gave himself up for her."

Some marriages end when hardship arises; they do not wait for their spouse to die. During challenging times, many marriages dissolve rather than couples trying to work things out. You have stood before man and God and said, "For better or for worse, for richer or for poorer, in sickness and in health, to love and to cherish, from this day forward until death do us part." For richer and for poorer is a part of hardship; it does not mean divorce. For example, when your spouse loses a job, has an injury, or becomes sick, this is the time you stand by your mate, encourage, comfort, and get help if needed, not a divorce.

Grieving does not have a timeline; it is complex and has no set schedule. It could take months, even years, to go through the grieving process. We have a grief session at our church. I attended the first grief classes that we had. It is an eight-week session, and at the end, you graduate. It did help me to be able to cope with my grief. If there is a family member or friend who you trust and can confide in, by all means, talk with them and express your feelings.

You are on a roller coaster when it comes to grieving. It is an emotional, physical, and psychological change that affects individuals differently. Grief does not disappear; it transforms into other ways. You can hear a song, different words, and even their voice, and start to cry. Sometimes I find myself talking to my mom's picture and can hear her answer me back.

You can glorify God and still grieve. If you read your Bible, you will see how God acknowledges those who mourn. Matthew 5:4: "Blessed are those who mourn, for they shall be comforted." Psalm 34:18: "The Lord is close to the brokenhearted and saves those who are crushed in spirit." Romans 12:15: "Rejoice with those who rejoice, and weep with those who weep." And 2 Corinthians 1:3-4: "Praise be to the God and Father of our Lord Jesus Christ, the Father of compassion and the God of all comfort, who comforts us in all our troubles, so that we can comfort those in any trouble with the comfort we ourselves receive from God." He comforts and blesses them that mourn. The Bible tells us that those who mourn will be comforted.

# CHAPTER 12

# *What I Would Tell My Younger Self Before Getting Married*

WHAT WOULD I TELL MY younger self before I got married? First, I would say to myself that love is a commitment, not a feeling. Before you get married, make sure you both have open, honest communication. Pray before you commit to anything. Before you get married, make sure you understand each other's values and goals and how he or she will handle conflict. You both need to be willing to accept change and grow together. Just because you disagree, you do not have to go your separate ways. I would tell my younger self a lot of things to watch out for if I ever fell in love again. I would be on the lookout for red flags so that I wouldn't get hurt again.

God had His own ideas for me. Darnell and I are total opposites. We have nothing in common but God. I grew up in the Christian church; his family was Jehovah's Witnesses. There was a bit of uncertainty; remember, he asked me to marry him three times before I said yes. My crazy sister told me if he asked again after my second no, "Girl, three strikes and you are out. He is handsome, and you are ugly, and he might change his mind." To know my sister is to love her. Then she wanted to know what took me so long.

Even though we did not have premarital counseling, our wedding coordinator was one. She did everything according to the Bible. She sat down and spoke with us, and what she said was extremely helpful. She told us to learn communication skills to help us talk with each other and be willing to listen. Premarital counseling helps you understand the different roles, your life goals, and responsibilities, and identify potential conflict areas. Your relationship will last with a powerful foundation and by putting God first.

Thank God, emotions did not cloud my judgment; I was able to reason and make good decisions. I did not misinterpret the information given to me. He just left a lot out. I found out after marriage that he was carrying a lot of baggage. He had a lot going on in his life that came to light after we got married: jail, court, and ladies. This is when my emotions began to change. I was not some girl off the street, and certain things I was not going to put up with.

I did not mistake attention for love. I know attention can be easily mistaken for love. Since I did not receive attention or love from Ray, I was not looking for it with Darnell. We did things together, such as dinner, movies, walks, and just talking, but that was not the reason I fell in love with him. It was the connection, his respect for me, his trust, and his presence when I needed him. Looking back now, my love for Ray was real, but his love for me was not. If things had not turned out the way they did, well, who knows? But it was God. God had and has His own agenda for me.

You might ask, "God, is this man (woman) for me?" Please wait and listen for God's answer. Ask God for a clear sign or confirmation that you are making the right decision. If they are the right person, ask God for wisdom, understanding, and discernment. Whatever God's plan is, follow it for your life. Pray that the man (or woman) will not hinder you from the plans God has for you and pray that the woman (or man) would be willing to help you grow stronger with God on your side. Pray that they will help you reach your goals and not hinder you. That your relationship will be at peace and healthy, and that you both will avoid people-pleasing and listening to what others have to say about your partner.

At the time of our marriage, I lacked discernment, but shortly after, I gained it. With discernment, I recognized the true Word of God, not misleading teaching or anything that could harm me. I was able to resist temptation. So discernment did not fail me. I was able to see right through my husband and his lies. Do not get me wrong; he was good at lying.

Godly preparation for marriage means each of you has a strong personal relationship with God. Fellowshipping with others who believe in God. You also have a strong foundation in the Bible and faith in God. My godly preparation for marriage came from my parents, grandmother, and sisters. They kept me on track until I gave my heart to the Lord.

While considering marriage, study and pray on these passages alone and with the person you're engaged to:

Genesis 2:24: "This is why a man leaves his father and mother and is united to his wife, and they become one flesh."

1 Corinthians 13:4-7: "Love is patient, love is kind. It does not envy, it does not boast, it is not proud. It does not dishonor others; it is not self-seeking. It is not easily angered; it keeps no record of wrongs. Love does not delight in evil but rejoices with the truth. It always protects, always trusts, always hopes, always perseveres."

Ephesians 5:21-33: "Submit to one another out of reverence for Christ. Wives, submit yourselves to your own husbands as you do to the Lord. For the husband is the head of the church, his body, of which he is the Savior. Now, as the church submits to Christ, so also wives should submit to their husbands in everything. Husbands, love your wives, just as Christ loved the church and gave himself up for her to make her holy, cleansing her by the washing with water through the word, and to present her to himself as a radiant church, without stain or wrinkle or any other blemish, but holy and blameless. In this same way, husbands ought to love their wives as their own bodies. He who loves his wife loves himself. After all, no one ever hated their own body, but they feed and care for their body, just as Christ does the church, for we are members of his body. For this reason, a man will leave his father and mother and be united to his wife, and the two will become one flesh. This is a profound mystery, but I am talking about Christ and the church. However, each one of you also must love his wife as he loves himself, and the wife must respect her husband."

John 15:12-13: "My command is this: Love each other as I have loved you. Greater love has no one than this: to lay down one's life for one's friends."

Matthew 18:21-22: "Then Peter came to Jesus and asked, 'Lord, how many times shall I forgive my brother or sister who sins against me? Up to seven times?' Jesus answered, 'I tell you, not seven times, but seventy-seven times.'"

Proverbs 3:5-6: "Trust in the Lord with all your heart and lean not on your own understanding; in all your ways submit to him, and he will make your paths straight."

Counseling is necessary and helpful in many ways. It will help you resolve conflicts, and both of you will learn how to communicate with each other. It will help you to deal with marriage challenges. Above all, use the strategies in the Bible as you determine who you should marry. Pray. Fast. Seek wise counsel. Seek God's Kingdom first, and always. Be equally yoked. Study together. Live individually and together for Christ. Stand firm in the marital vows, let "'til God do us part" be the goal and the blessing.

# A PRAYER FOR MARRIAGES

D EAR HEAVENLY FATHER, I COME before your throne asking you to bless every married couple. I pray for your grace and mercy, and for divine blessings for all married couples to withstand challenges, so that no storm will come crashing or threatening to break up any marriage. Help us to remember the love and respect we have for one another, so that nothing can come between us. Please keep us in your Word so we can weather any storm that comes our way. We know that if the devil cannot get you one way, he will try another. Lord, he will try you on your job, finances, children, church, and will try to come between you and your spouse. Lord, we already know that no weapon formed against us shall prosper.

Lord, if any marriages are struggling, I ask for healing and restoration. I know that you are the God who can heal broken marriages, the brokenhearted, and bind up wounds. You are a God of love, peace, forgiveness, and long-suffering. Teach us to have patience, faith, consideration, kindness, and love for one another. Please help us to overcome any adversities and protect our relationships from any external threats. If any marriages need to be restored, I ask that you restore each marriage.

All these things I ask in your Son Jesus' Name, Amen.

# ABOUT BONITA
# L. REYNOLDS

Bonita L. Reynolds draws from a deep well of life experience in her writing. She and her husband, Darnell, will soon celebrate 48 years of a faith-centered marriage. Their legacy includes a loving family of three children, three grandchildren, and three great-grandchildren, all active in their shared church community. Professionally, Bonita has dedicated her life to service, with a distinguished career spanning over 30 years in the medical field and 22 years in early childhood education, during which she focused on creating safe and stimulating environments for children to thrive.

www.ingramcontent.com/pod-product-compliance
Lightning Source LLC
Chambersburg PA
CBHW040823120726
48005CB00012B/1497